JACQUES PEPIN
TODAY'S GOURMET

We gratefully acknowledge the following sponsors
of the public television series *TODAY'S GOURMET:*

Managing Editor
LINDA BRANDT

Book & Photo Designer
BERNIE SCHIMBKE

Typographer
NED TAKAHASHI

Photographer
NIKOLAY ZÛREK

Food Stylist
BERNIE SCHIMBKE

Chef
AMY MCKENZIE

Cover Designer
ADRIAN MORGAN

Cover Photographer
PENINA

Print Coordinator
INTERPRINT

Props Provided By:
PIERRE DEUX
HILARY THATZ
CRATE & BARREL
MACYS CALIFORNIA, INC.

Pictured on page 1: Grilled Chicken with Cabbage Anchoyade; Tomato, Onion & Parsley Vinaigrette and
Hot Shrimp on Spinach. Pictured on page 2: Raspberry Granité and Grapes & Raisins in Lime Cookie Cone.

Library of Congress Card Number: 90-92204
ISBN 0-912333-08-1
Manufactured in the United States of America; color pages done in Hong Kong.
10 9 8 7
Distributed to the trade by Publishers Group West.

"In the history of cooking, no cuisine has ever remained alive and vital without being closely associated with health."

The production of TODAY'S GOURMET, the television series as well as the cookbook, required a concerted effort on the part of many, many capable people, and I would like to thank everyone involved with these projects for their support and hard work. It is impossible to name every person associated with all the various facets of the show and book, but the people I especially want to thank are:

Marjorie Poore, my executive producer at KQED, for her indefatigable drive to find sponsorship for the show, and the confidence this reflected in me; Peter Stein, my producer, for his vision and cooperation; Linda Brandt, my associate producer, who worked diligently on both the show and the book; Katherine Russell, my capable director; Susie Heller, my culinary advisor and dear friend, for her enthusiasm and hard work; Bernie Schimbke, who ably directed set and food styling; Ken Short, for his outstanding set design; and of course, Dan Bowe, my great back kitchen supervisor, and his wonderful staff: Travis Brady, Jeff Forman, Robin Margolin, Amy McKenzie, and Michael Pollock.

JACQUES PEPIN

· TABLE OF CONTENTS ·

· INTRODUCTION ·

"This is a sensitive and sensible way to cook, a cooking style that emphasizes aspects of health in a common-sense way . . . yet still exhibits elegance and joy in its creation."

When I recall the food that we used to serve at Le Pavillon in New York thirty years ago when I first came to the United States, I realize how much cooking in general has changed and improved, especially in the last twenty or so years.

I like to think that my cooking has changed a great deal, too. Through the years, I have tried to keep abreast of what's going on and have made adjustments in my cooking to accommodate such changes as those brought about by the social up-heavals of the 60's and 70's, spanning everything from women's liberation to organic gardening–one offshoot of a tremendous national concern about health.

Paradoxically, it is interesting to note that the current preoccupation with health as it relates to food is not a new or revolutionary phenomenon. Dating back as far as the ancient Greek poet and gastronome, Archestratus, and the Romans, and continuing on through the cooking of the 16th, 17th and 18th centuries, food has always been closely associated with health.

In fact, most cookbooks prior to the l9th century were gastro-medical in nature, and there are early 20th century examples of these as well: a book by Dr. Edouard de Pomaine, published during World War II, dealt with healthful eating in times when food supplies were scarce.

The trend today is a return to that basic notion of health encapsulated in Brillat-Savarin's aphorism stating "you are what you eat." The same notion was expressed later by Thomas Alva Edison, who said, "The doctor of the future will give no medicine, but will educate his patients in the care of the human frame, in diet, and in the cause and preven-tion of disease."

The concerns of modern, well-educated eaters parallel those of modern, well-educated young

·INTRODUCTION·

"The concerns of modern, well-educated eaters parallel those of modern, well-educated young chefs and go beyond how food tastes and how it is presented ... The quality of the products in our diet directly affects the quality of our health and the health of our families."

chefs and go beyond how food tastes and how it is presented. Today's astute food buyer wants produce that is not only fresh, but is free of chemicals. The quality of the products in our diet directly affects the quality of our health and the health of our families. We have to stay in tune with nature; if the chickens we eat feed on grass and natural grains in an area free of pesticides and insecticides, their quality and the quality of the eggs they produce will be substantially better.

Health concerns me greatly in *TODAY'S GOURMET*. Although this is not intended to be a low-calorie, low-fat, low-sodium or low-cholesterol cookbook, the recipes here reflect how important I think it is to moderate these nutritional components. Keep in mind, however, that I am a cook, not a doctor. I am not a guru of macrobiotic food, insisting on the wholesomeness of grains and fiber, nor have I assumed the role of a nutritionist, advising people what they should or should not eat. Eating, for me, has always meant enjoyment and sharing, never obligation.

On these pages, I want to introduce you to a cuisine that demonstrates a rational approach to cooking. This is a sensitive and sensible way to cook, a cooking style that emphasizes aspects of health in a common-sense way–a diverse diet with more fiber and less saturated fat, more fish and shellfish, smaller portions of well-trimmed meat, vegetables cooked in a manner that preserves vitamins and nutrients–yet still exhibits elegance and joy in its creation. This is the cuisine of today and the cuisine of tomorrow, and it represents a lower-calorie, healthier, faster and simpler way of cooking.

In a true reflection of life, some of the recipes are more concerned with health than others. When we join with friends and family on holidays and special occasions, we sometimes don't count calories–we

· INTRODUCTION ·

indulge. At other times, we are more careful. I still use butter, salt, and cream, although parsimoniously, adding them in small amounts at the moment when they most influence taste. Essentially, this is modern cooking–a blend of substance and sophistication, contemporary food that appeals to everyone.

This kind of cooking avoids gimmicks and trends, rather satisfies the tastes of a more discriminating audience while meeting their nutritional needs in a non-prescriptive way. I want a cuisine that appeals to the epicurean and the jogger/sports enthusiast as well as the home cook and the single professional. I even makes suggestions for people on special diets on how they can adapt my recipes to satisfy their personal requirements.

As a professional chef, I also want to teach proper cooking techniques by demonstrating how these techniques can save time and effort and so make cooking that much more enjoyable. My cuisine is not a complicated or contrived mix of esoteric ingredients, and it is not intended for an elitist group of people. It is for everyone. Everyone should know how to defat a stock, how to trim a piece of meat properly, and how to healthfully prepare beef, pork, and other foods not usually associated with lighter cuisine.

Finally, I want to show the importance of togetherness, convivality and *joie de vivre* in the kitchen. Cooking should be exciting–nothing compares to the enjoyment of sharing good food while spending time with family and friends. But most of all, I hope that the knowledge readers gain from *TODAY'S GOURMET* will make their lives richer, healthier, and happier.

· MENUS ·

On the following pages I have listed the twenty-six different menus that are featured on my current television series, *TODAY'S GOURMET.* Any sort of recipe grouping is arbitrary, however, influenced by such factors as market considerations and personal food preferences.

Use my listings merely as a point of departure. Reorganize as you wish, extrapolating a recipe from one menu and adding it to another.

Although there aren't any salad recipes in the book, you'll note that I have listed them on most of my menus. We eat salads every day, and I recommend them for taste and because they help balance a diet. Bread and wine are also part of our daily fare. If you include them with your meals as well, remember to take into account the added calories.

Although we don't have dessert on a daily basis at home, preferring to end our meals with fresh fruits, I have included dessert recipes here to complete the menus and make them special enough to serve when you entertain.

· MENUS ·

MY MOTHER'S FAVORITES

This menu gives me a homey feeling. The garlic soup, containing potatoes and leeks, and the roast of veal, cooked in a Dutch oven with artichokes and lots of garlic, remind me of my youth in France. The almond cake dessert, originally called *pain de Gênes* or "bread of Genoa", usually is very rich, calling for lots of egg yolks and butter. But in my version, I have reduced the number of calories in the cake and substituted a flavorful mango coulis for the traditional rich custard sauce.

Garlic Soup (page 26)

Veal Roast with Artichokes (page 84)

Salad

Almond Cake with Mango Coulis (page 124)

·

MEDITERRANEAN FLAVORS

In this menu, I have tried to capture the diverse flavors of the Mediterranean Basin. I begin with tuna tartare served on a bed of marinated cucumbers, which suggests regions of Italy or the South of France. Next comes a classic dish–in fact one might call it the national dish of Spain–*paella*. Saffron-flavored rice is combined with pieces of hot sausage, chicken, an assortment of shellfish and of course, fresh vegetables. For dessert, I have chosen figs poached in a spicy port sauce. It reminds me of Portugal with a touch of Italy thrown in, because after all, I do use Campari in the sauce.

Tuna Tartare on Marinated Cucumbers (page 52)

Chicken & Seafood Paella (page 66)

Salad

Calimyrna Figs in Spicy Port Sauce (page 137)

· MENUS ·

NOUVELLE CUISINE

This menu features robust, lusty dishes characteristic of nouvelle cuisine–very fresh ingredients, quickly cooked light sauces and interesting combinations of food with great eye appeal. In the first course, the potato crepe is thicker than a conventional one, more like a pancake, and it is garnished with two different types of caviar, sour cream and herbs. Grilled chicken breast, without skin and thinly sliced, is served on a bed of shredded cabbage seasoned with anchovies, garlic and olive oil. I finish the menu with a deliciously light chocolate cake served with a concentrated raspberry-rum sauce.

Potato Crepes with Caviar (page 46)

Grilled Chicken with Cabbage Anchoyade (page 70)

Salad

Chocolate Soufflé Cake with Raspberry-Rum Sauce (page 133)

·

A PARTY MENU

This type of menu makes life easier when you invite a group of friends over for a casual party. The braised leeks with tomatoes are best served at room temperature so they are perfect in a buffet setting. This is true, too, of the smoked pork shoulder roast with mustard-honey glaze. I place it on the buffet table along with a sharp knife and let guests help themselves. A bowl of braised cabbage is set out as an accompaniment, as well as a simple salad. And for dessert, strawberry shortcake is always a hit. You can assemble it in advance or bring everything to the table and let guests serve themselves.

Leeks with Tomato & Olive Oil (page 39)

Smoked Pork Roast with Mustard-Honey Glaze (page 93)

Braised Sour Cabbage (page 98)

Salad

Buttermilk Strawberry Shortcakes (page 152)

· MENUS ·

COOKING AGAINST THE CLOCK

If you cook in the following sequence, this interesting menu can be ready in half an hour. Begin by making the bulgar. While it cooks, prepare the pineapple and let it macerate in the liqueur. Then grill the lamb chops and as they cook, begin the first course by sautéing the damp greens. Arrange them on plates. Next remove the cooked lamb and let it rest in a warm oven. Then sauté the shrimp and arrange over the greens. Finish the bulgar and prepare the tomato salad. Finally, finish and serve the lamb chops and complete the pineapple dessert.

Hot Shrimp on Spinach (page 55)

Grilled Savory Lamb Chops (page 87)

Curried Bulgar with Currants (page 104)

Tomato, Onion & Parsley Vinaigrette (page 96)

Salpicon of Pineapple (page 148)

EARTHY COUNTRY COOKING

This hearty menu begins with a gratin of scallions. Although made with half-and-half, it is still relatively low in fat. The same is true with the delicious ragout of rabbit. Another grain to give variety to your repertoire of complex carbohydrates is cornmeal and this version, flavored with Gruyère, is no exception. A salad is next, followed by a fresh fruit fondue with a delightful apricot dipping sauce.

Gratin of Scallions (page 42)

Ragout of Rabbit (page 82)

Cornmeal au Gruyère (page 105)

Salad

Fresh Fruit with Minted Apricot Fondue (page 138)

· MENUS ·

BISTRO COOKING OF NEW YORK

Although a bit more trendy than most French bistro food, New York bistro food is somewhat similar. Young chefs everywhere–and especially in New York–are interested in a lighter, more imaginative cuisine, one that will satisfy not only the epicurean, but the average person who wants to eat flavorful food without feeling guilty. The eggplant rolls contain many different vegetables combined with fresh, spicy seasonings. Cooked between layers of sliced potato, the red snapper remains moist and crisp. Following a salad, I finish with my interpretation of a classic bistro dish, apple tart.

Sautéed Eggplant Rolls (page 41)

Red Snapper in Potato Jackets (page 61)

Salad

Baked Apple Tart (page 125)

·

A HEARTY SUPPER

This is a meal to come home to on a cold night! Begin with clam croquettes, followed by a favorite of mine, meat and vegetables that have been braised together until all their juices blend. To the well-trimmed pork, I add dried tomatoes, onions, garlic and carrots, all of which lend appealing flavor to the cooking juices. The zucchini-sauced pasta complements the main course. Next comes a salad, followed by the perfect conclusion, caramelized apple timbales.

Clam Croquettes (page 48)

Braised Pork Cocotte (page 92)

Pasta with Zucchini Sauce (page 43)

Salad

Caramelized Apple Timbales (page 126)

· MENUS ·

THE HEALTHY GOURMET

Here is a menu that concentrates on lowering calories. In fact, the total calorie count for the entire meal is about 700 calories per person, with less than 22 per cent of these coming from fat. Braised with lemon juice, the steamed endives are a refreshing first course selection. Poached chicken is served with an assortment of vegetables, and the concentrated broth, with croutons. After a salad, I offer dessert–a large, cone-shaped cookie filled with grapes and dried currants or raisins.

Steamed Endive in Lemon Juice (page 40)

Chicken Consommé with Croutons (page 75)

Poule au Pot (page 75)

Salad

Grapes & Raisins in Lime Cookie Cones (page 143)

·

POTPOURRI DINNER

This menu is interesting because it combines a new style of dishes that have become popular in the last few years. Beef carpaccio, a re-interpretation of steak tartare, is great to serve for supper or for an after-the-theatre party. You can make it ahead and it is always well received. Thick, fleshy catfish, served on a bed of fiber-rich ratatouille, is a very satisfying main course followed by a simple salad of mixed greens. And then comes dessert–a wonderful hazelnut parfait.

Beef Carpaccio (page 57)

Catfish on Ratatouille (page 65)

Salad

Hazelnut Parfait with Candied Violets (page 144)

· MENUS ·

HOLIDAY TRADITIONS

We splurge a little over the holidays and expand our menu, but even so, at 1200 calories per serving, this meal is conservative compared to most holiday fare. Garnished with snow peas and red pepper, the first-course scallop dish is colorful and original. Oven-roasted turkey contains a mushroom stuffing made with wholewheat bread and the ginger-flavored carrot purée makes a delightful accompaniment. Our double holiday dessert–chocolate mint truffles and candied orange rind–offers a festive finish to this holiday menu.

Sautéed Scallops with Snow Peas (page 54)

Roasted Turkey with Mushroom Stuffing (page 80)

Carrot Purée with Ginger (page 103)

Salad

Chocolate Mint Truffles (page 132)

Candied Orange Rind (page 153)

·

BIG TASTE ON A SMALL BUDGET

Here is a menu that emphasizes economy in the kitchen. I love to make vegetable soup and finish it with pasta such as vermicelli. It takes only a few minutes and is a great vehicle for using leftover vegetables–something that I always have in my refrigerator. The main course consists of lean sausage meat wrapped in cabbage leaves, grilled and then served on a bed of lentils. And for the finale, try this delicious fruit dessert that combines baked pears and figs.

Potage de Légumes au Vermicelli (page 28)

Saucisses au Chou on Lentils (page 90)

Salad

Baked Pears with Figs (page 149)

· MENUS ·

COOKING FOR THE FAMILY

Because much of this meal can be prepared ahead, including the colorful chocolate cups filled with nuts and bits of fruit, it is a great menu to cook with the family on weekends. Kids love to help make potato pancakes. These are filled with a flavorful mushroom mixture. The main course, veal chops served with a simple corn and red pepper sauté, is always a hit. And don't forget to include the family when making dessert. Pieces of fresh and dried fruit, nuts and seeds are pressed into small cups of melted chocolate. When they harden, peel off the paper wrappers and serve.

Mushroom-stuffed Potato Pancakes (page 45)
Veal Chops with Mushrooms (page 83)
Corn & Pepper Sauté (page 101)
Salad
Chocolate & Fruit Nut Cups (page 131)

·

SPRING ELEGANCE

Celebrate spring with this elegant, well-balanced menu. All of the vegetables–peas, carrots, asparagus–plus the fresh strawberries served in a deliciously light "floating island" dessert, provide a wonderful source of fiber, complex carbohydrates and vitamins. Even the beef roast meets the recommended daily allowance of no more than one-third of our calorie intake coming from fat.

Asparagus in Mustard Sauce (page 33)
Spicy Beef Shell Roast (page 86)
Carotte Ciboulette (page 102)
Peas à la Française (page 99)
Pistachio Floating Island with Blackcurrant Sauce (page 150)

· MENUS ·

COOKING FOR FRIENDS

Cooking for friends is a great pleasure for me and here is one of my favorite menus. I begin by serving steamed cod on tapenade, followed by *poulet au vin rouge*. The classic chicken dish is garnished with mushrooms, glazed shallots and croutons, and is served with a garlic-flavored potato and turnip mixture. To conclude, I serve fresh blueberries topped with plain yogurt and a sprinkling of brown sugar. The brown sugar melts through the yogurt, creating a nice design.

Steamed Cod on Tapenade (page 50)

Poulet au Vin Rouge (page 76)

Turnips & Mashed Potatoes (page 109)

Salad

Blueberries with Brown Sugar (page 129)

·

COUNTRY FRENCH/BELGIAN MENU

Combining mussels and fried potatoes is actually Belgian in derivation but my "French" family really enjoys this combination, too. Where I live, mussels are plentiful and inexpensive in the summertime, so when temperatures soar, we prefer to cook both the mussels and the French fries outdoors. Another family favorite, braised stuffed artichokes, is a nice accompaniment. For dessert, we all enjoy a light version of traditional coffee creme caramel.

Braised Stuffed Artichokes (page 32)

Moules Maison (page 60)

French Fries (page 107)

Salad

Coffee Creme Caramel (page 134)

· MENUS ·

CASUAL & SIMPLE

An interesting composite of different tastes, textures and colors highlights this flavorful menu. For starters, fresh vegetable sauce over pasta is a healthy, high-fiber alternative to more common pasta sauces made with butter and cream. Next, I like to marinate well-trimmed leg of lamb in a pungent sauce, then grill it and serve with a scallion and cauliflower dish. And for dessert, I make a cherry bread pudding, assembled and baked in a gratin dish and flavored with almonds.

Pasta with Fresh Vegetable Sauce (page 44)
Grilled Leg of Lamb (page 89)
Cauliflower in Scallion Sauce (page 100)
Salad
Cherry Bread Pudding (page 130)

·

A SAVORY BREAKFAST

In this menu, you will find many different recipes, some with variations. Although I have provided more than you would want to serve for any one breakfast or brunch, the menu gives you an idea of what can be prepared for a savory type of breakfast, rather than one containing an abundance of sweets. There are three variations of the basic *oeuf cocotte*, a smoked whitefish mold, flavorful oatmeal-leek soup, a classic mushroom omelet, hearty buttermilk bread and a fruit dish combining grapefruit and orange segments.

Oeuf Cocotte (page 110)
Smoked Whitefish Mold (page 49)
Oatmeal Leek Soup (page 31)
Mushroom Omelet (page 111)
Orange & Grapefruit Segments (page 135)

· MENUS ·

LIGHT & LEISURELY

This elegant menu emphasizes speed in the kitchen, speed that is based, at least most of the time, on a thorough understanding of the dishes you are about to prepare. The first course contrasts pink-colored salmon against the green of fresh spinach and makes for a beautiful presentation. And what a great mixture of vegetables in the chicken dish, from mushrooms and garlic to shallots and yams. After the salad comes a simple ending to this well-balanced meal– a baked banana dessert served with a zesty lemon sauce.

Sautéed Salmon on Greens (page 51)

Chicken Legs with Wine & Yams (page 68)

Salad

Baked Bananas in Lemon-Rum Sauce (page 128)

GREAT SANDWICHES

A menu of great-tasting sandwiches can be varied ad infinitum. Sandwiches are a great way to use cold cuts, leftover meats, fish or even vegetables. They can be complex as in a *pan bagna,* with many vegetables, or as simple as James Beard's onion sandwiches. And they are versatile– serve them at any meal, as well as on picnics or buffets. Good cooks know that the most essential component of any sandwich is the bread. This high-gluten bread, which can easily be made in the food processor, is wonderfully adaptable and depending on the grain and flour you use, the variations are endless.

Rolls & Baguettes (page 112)

Roasted Eggplant Sandwiches (page 118)

Olive & Tomato Toasts (page 119)

James Beard's Onion Sandwiches (page 116)

Pan Bagna (page 120)

Smoked Salmon & Cucumber Sandwiches (page 117)

Jam "Sandwiches" (page 121)

· MENUS ·

CLASSIC & CHIC

The food in this menu is delicious as well as beautiful to look at. Don't be afraid to use unusual ingredients such as sunflower seeds or quinoa, a delightful grain that is very high in protein. Although quail and fresh trout may sound a bit esoteric, you will be surprised at how easy they are to prepare with terrific results. Following the salad, the menu ends with a raspberry granité, a concentrated sherbet made with raspberry purée. It provides the perfect finish to this meal.

Trout Sauté Terry (page 53)

Grilled Quail (page 79)

Quinoa with Sunflower Seeds (page 79)

Salad

Raspberry Granité (page 151)

BISTRO COOKING OF LYON

Bistro cooking implies casualness and sophistication at the same time. The setting is usually simple, while the food–although comfortable, recognizable and familiar–is a bit more sophisticated than you would prepare at home. I think that those little unpretentious restaurants called *bistrots* in Lyon serve the most authentic French cooking you can find in France. For the first course, I combine beans with broccoli de rapé, which is part of the mustard greens family. With the main steak dish, I serve sautéed potatoes, followed by a salad. I finish with a refreshing baked apricot dessert.

Beans & Broccoli de Rapé (page 34)

Wine Merchant Steak (page 85)

Pommes Persillade (page 108)

Salad

Baked Apricots with Almonds (page 127)

· MENUS ·

AROUND-THE-WORLD MENU

This menu is diverse, composed of dishes from around the world that work well together. The crabmeat cakes come from the southern United States, although I've given them an unusual twist with the addition of an avocado sauce. Irish lamb stew is a classic. Made from either lamb shoulder or leg of lamb, it includes a wide assortment of simmering vegetables. Following a salad, I like to serve an interesting dessert of dried figs studded with fresh almonds, similar to those found in the markets of southern Portugal.

Crab Cakes with Avocado Sauce (page 47)

Irish Lamb Stew (page 88)

Salad

Figs Villamora (page 136)

LOW-CAL STEAMED DINNER

Weight watchers will like this special menu because it contains fewer than 600 calories per serving and less than 26 per cent of that total is from fat. And everything cooks together in about a half an hour. You can prepare the salmon and the two side dishes in a three-tiered steamer, staggering the cooking times. I begin steaming the potatoes. After they cook for about 15 minutes, I start the broccoli. Finally, after the vegetables have cooked a while longer, I steam the salmon. There is even time to assemble two sauces–one for the salmon and one for the broccoli–and make dessert.

Salmon Pojarski (page 62)

Pommes Anglaises (page 106)

Broccoli Piquante (page 97)

Salad

Oranges in Grand Marnier (page 145)

· MENUS ·

THE THRIFTY KITCHEN

The dishes featured here would not be served together. Instead, this "menu" exemplifies the concept of economy in the kitchen, demonstrating what can be done with different parts of a chicken. Three of the recipes are made with chicken parts that you might ordinarily discard–the skin, the carcass and the gizzard. Perhaps the most sophisticated dish on the menu, chicken served in a tarragon-flavored sauce, is made with the breast and leg meat, which is poached in white wine and finished with a tarragon cream. Interestingly enough, this dish has fewer calories than any of the others because it is poached in wine rather than sautéed in fat. And the amount of cream added is negligible, amounting to only l tablespoon, or 45 calories per person.

Split Pea Soup with Cracklings (page 29)

Brown Rice Chicken Fricassee (page 78)

Chicken in Tarragon Sauce (page 69)

Salad

Fruit Medley

·

NEW ENGLAND SUMMER SUPPER

In the summer along the coast of Connecticut we eat a lot of lobster, usually steaming it and serving it with corn on the cob and potatoes. Sometimes, however, I like to incorporate lobster into a more elegant menu. In this recipe lobster is made with couscous, a quick-cooking granulated wheat that cooks up fluffy and tender. Instead of a caloric butter sauce, I serve it with a delicate chive sauce made from the reduced cooking stock, a little olive oil and minced chives. The smooth chicken and spinach-flavored *velouté* makes a satisfying first course and for dessert, we have individual crepe soufflés served with a tangy grapefruit sauce.

Chicken & Spinach Velouté (page 27)

Couscous of Lobster (page 64)

Salad

Crepes Soufflés in Grapefruit Sauce (page 146)

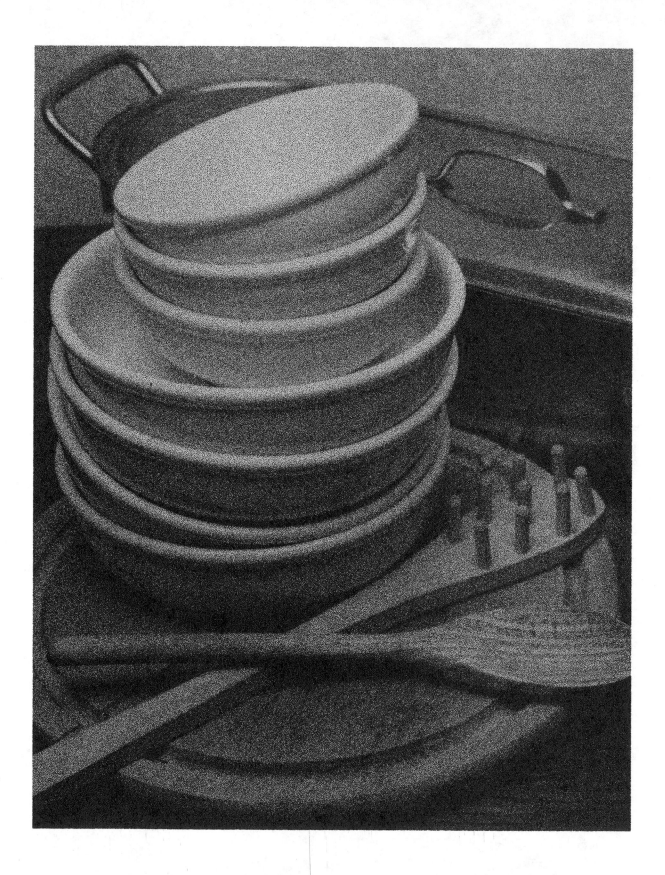

· FIRST COURSE ·

Garlic Soup
Chicken & Spinach Velouté
Potage de Légumes au Vermicelli
Split Pea Soup with Cracklings
Chicken Broth
Oatmeal Leek Soup
Braised Stuffed Artichokes
Asparagus in Mustard Sauce
Beans & Broccoli de Rapé
Leeks with Tomato & Olive Oil
Steamed Endive in Lemon Juice
Sautéed Eggplant Rolls
Gratin of Scallions
Pasta & Zucchini
Pasta with Fresh Vegetable Sauce
Mushroom-Stuffed Potato Pancakes
Potato Crepes with Caviar
Crab Cakes with Avocado Sauce
Clam Croquettes
Smoked Whitefish Mold
Steamed Cod on Tapenade
Sautéed Salmon on Greens
Tuna Tartare on Marinated Cucumbers
Trout Sauté Terry
Sautéed Scallops with Snow Peas
Hot Shrimp on Spinach
Mussels Gratinee
Beef Carpaccio

GARLIC SOUP

Along with some leek and onion, there is a lot of garlic in this soup. Cooked as it is here in liquid, however, its flavor is quite subtle, even mild. As a thickening agent, I use potato, although the same soup can be thickened with leftover bread, couscous or cornmeal instead. My mother used to finish this soup with cream, but I use milk; the result is wonderfully satisfying.

1	leek (about 4 oz.)
1	onion (about 4 oz.)
2	tablespoons peanut oil
8	cloves garlic, peeled and crushed (about 2 tbs.)
2	cups unsalted chicken stock, preferably homemade (see Chicken Broth, page 30)
2	cups water
1	pound potatoes, peeled and cut into 2-inch chunks
1	teaspoon salt
½	teaspoon freshly ground black pepper
2	slices white bread
1	tablespoon canola oil
1	cup milk

1) Trim the leek, wash it well, and cut it into 1-inch pieces. (You should have about 1 cup.) Peel and coarsely chop the onion.

2) Heat the peanut oil in a saucepan and when hot, add the leeks, onions and garlic, and sauté for 2 minutes. Then add the stock, water, potatoes, salt and pepper, and bring to a boil. Cover, reduce the heat to low, and boil gently for 25 minutes.

3) Meanwhile, remove the crusts from the bread and cut it into ½-inch croutons. (You should have 1¼ cups.) Moisten the croutons with the vegetable oil and spread them on a cookie sheet. Place in a preheated 400° oven for 8 to 10 minutes, until nicely browned.

4) When the soup is cooked, strain it through a sieve, retaining the liquid. Place the solids in the bowl of a food processor and process until smooth. Return to the saucepan with the reserved liquid and add the milk. Bring to a boil and serve with the croutons.

Yield: 4 servings (6 cups)

CHICKEN & SPINACH VELOUTE

The quality of this soup depends on the quality of the chicken stock used. Homemade chicken stock should be completely defatted and highly concentrated. Although I thicken it with Cream of Wheat, which cooks quite quickly, you can use cornmeal as well as tapioca or semolina, any of which would work equally well.

4   cups unsalted chicken stock, preferably homemade (see Chicken Broth, page 30)
1   cup water
¾   teaspoon salt
¼   teaspoon freshly ground black pepper
6   tablespoons instant Cream of Wheat
6   ounces spinach, stems removed and washed
⅓   cup heavy cream

1) Bring the stock, water, salt and pepper to a boil in a stainless steel saucepan. Add the Cream of Wheat, mix well, bring back to the boil, and cook gently for 3 minutes.

2) Cut the washed spinach very coarsely and add it to the pan. Bring back to the boil and boil for 2 minutes. Stir in the cream and serve immediately.

Yield: 4 servings

POTAGE DE LEGUMES AU VERMICELLI

Although I serve this hearty soup as a first course, it would also make a satisfying light supper on its own with the addition of a crunchy bread, a salad and a piece of cheese to finish the meal. (Pictured on page 36.)

1	tablespoon virgin olive oil
½	tablespoon unsalted butter
1	leek (about 3 oz.), trimmed of damaged leaves, cleaned, and cut into ½-inch pieces
1	medium onion (about 4 oz.), peeled and coarsely chopped
2	carrots (about 4 oz.), peeled and cut into ½-inch pieces
1	zucchini (about 4 oz.), trimmed and cut into ¾-inch pieces
4	mushrooms (4 oz.), coarsely chopped (1 cup)
1	yam (about 6 oz.), peeled and cut into ½-inch pieces
7	cups water
1	teaspoon salt
¼	teaspoon freshly ground black pepper
1	cup vermicelli (angel hair pasta) or very thin noodles (about ¾ oz.)

1) Heat the oil and butter in a saucepan. When hot, add the leeks and onions and sauté for 2 minutes. Then add the carrots, zucchini, mushrooms and yams, and mix well. Add the water, salt and pepper.

2) Bring to a boil, cover, reduce the heat and boil gently for about 12 minutes.

3) Add the pasta, bring back to the boil and cook, covered, for about 4 minutes. Serve.

Yield: 6 servings (8 cups)

MAKING SOUP
My choice of vegetables for this soup is based on what is available in my refrigerator. In addition, while I thicken the soup here with vermicelli (angel hair pasta), you could use another type of starch— from oatmeal to cous-cous, tapioca, or Cream of Wheat.

SPLIT PEA SOUP WITH CRACKLINGS

Split peas are extremely high in soluble fiber. This is a great winter recipe when served with crusty bread and a simple first-course salad. The soup can be frozen, although it might require additional water when reheated, since it tends to thicken when frozen.

6	ounces chicken skin cut into 1-inch pieces
2	medium onions (8 oz.), peeled and cut into 1-inch pieces
2	to 3 cloves garlic, peeled crushed and coarsely chopped
8	cups water
2	teaspoons herbes de Provence
2	teaspoons salt
½	teaspoon freshly ground black pepper
¼	teaspoon Tabasco sauce
1	pound dry split peas

1) Place the chicken skin pieces in a skillet and sauté over high heat for 8 to 10 minutes, until the fat is rendered and the skin is crisp. Remove the cracklings and fat and discard all but 3 tablespoons of the fat.

2) Place the reserved fat and cracklings in a large saucepan, add the onion, and sauté for 5 minutes. Then, add the garlic, mix well, and stir in the water, herbes de Provence, salt, pepper, Tabasco and split peas.

3) Bring to a boil, cover, reduce the heat and boil gently for 1 hour. Stir the soup well; although it should be fairly thick, if you would prefer it thinned a little, add some water.

4) To serve, divide the soup among six bowls, and offer extra Tabasco sauce, if desired.

Yield: 6 servings

MAKING CRACKLINGS

For the cracklings, I cook the chicken skin until it renders its fat and becomes crisp. I discard most of the cooking fat, retaining only 3 tablespoons, which I use to brown the onions for the soup. If you want to reduce your calorie intake further, eliminate the cracklings altogether and just use the chicken fat or 3 tablespoons of peanut oil to start your soup.

CHICKEN BROTH

There is nothing like the smell of a stock slowly cooking on the stove. Fresh stock is easy to make, inexpensive, and far better than any store-bought facsimile. It does require a little time, but the amount of work involved is minimal. Take advantage of a day at home to make stock; you can be doing other things while it cooks, and then you can strain, package, and freeze it for use when needed. It is well worth the time and effort.

3	pounds chicken backs and necks
5	quarts water
2	shallots
1	piece of ginger about the size of a large shallot
1	star anise
1	tablespoon herbes de Provence

1) Place the bones and water in a heavy pot and bring to a boil over high heat. Reduce the heat, and simmer for 15 minutes. Skim off and discard the fat and impurities.

2) Impale the shallots and ginger on a skewer and hold over a flame (or place under a broiler) for 4 to 5 minutes, turning occasionally, until black on all sides. Add to the stock to impart taste and color. Stir in the star anise and herbes de Provence, and boil gently for 2 hours, partially covered.

3) Strain, cool, and remove all fat from the surface, as directed below. Refrigerate or freeze.

Yield: 2 quarts

A WORD ABOUT STRAINING
The stock may be strained through paper towels to eliminate as much fat as possible. If time permits, it is a good idea to chill the stock until the fat solidifies on top. After it hardens, you can remove and discard this additional fat with ease.

OATMEAL LEEK SOUP

This soup can be prepared in a few minutes. I use whole milk, but you can use skimmed milk or something in-between if it better meets your calorie needs. You can substitute scallions for the leeks, too, and use cornmeal or farina to thicken the soup instead of oats.

1   small leek
3½ cups whole milk
¼   teaspoon freshly ground black
     pepper
½   teaspoon salt
1   cup quick-cooking oats

1) Trim the leek, wash it well and mince, to make about 1 cup.

2) In a saucepan, bring the leeks, milk, pepper and salt to a boil. Simmer for 2 minutes and then stir in the oats.

3) Cook for about 2 minutes. Serve immediately, or keep warm in a double boiler over warm water.

Note: (If the soup thickens, thin to desired consistency with milk or water.)

Yield: 4 servings

BRAISED STUFFED ARTICHOKES

Instead of stuffing these artichokes, you can serve them simply with a little olive oil and lemon juice. If you do this, however, increase the initial cooking time from 20 to 30 minutes for this size artichoke, since they won't be cooked additionally, as the stuffed ones are.

4	large artichokes (about 8 oz. each)
6	tablespoons virgin olive oil
2	medium onions (about 6 oz.), peeled and chopped
3	cloves garlic, peeled, crushed, and chopped (1½ tsp.)
6	ounces mushrooms, rinsed and coarsely chopped (1¾ cups)
3	slices white bread
¾	teaspoon salt
¾	teaspoon freshly ground black pepper
1	cup water

1) Prepare the artichokes as described below.

For stuffing:
1) Heat 4 tablespoons of the olive oil in a skillet and sauté the onions in the hot oil for about 1 minute. Add the garlic and mushrooms, and continue sautéeing for about 2 minutes.

2) Tear the bread slices into the bowl of a food processor and process for a few seconds, until crumbed. You should have about 1½ cups of crumbs. Add the bread crumbs to the mixture in the skillet and sauté for about 3 to 4 minutes, until nicely browned. Stir in ½ teaspoon each of the salt and pepper, and set aside.

3) When the artichokes are cool enough to handle, hold them upside down over the sink and squeeze out as much water as possible. Remove the thin center leaves to expose the chokes and discard. Cut off the stems and, if they are tender, chop them coarsely and add them to the stuffing. Fill the center of the artichokes with the stuffing and insert remaining stuffing between the leaves.

4) Place the stuffed artichokes upright in a saucepan and pour in the water, the remaining 2 tablespoons of olive oil, and ¼ teaspoon each of the salt and pepper. Bring to a boil, and boil gently, covered, for 15 minutes. If the pan becomes dry and the artichokes begin to fry, add 2 to 3 tablespoons of water. Arrange the artichokes on a serving plate and serve with any remaining natural juices.

Yield: 4 servings

PERFECT ARTICHOKES
With a large, sharp knife, trim about 1½ inches from the tops of the artichokes. Using scissors, cut off the thorny top third of the remaining leaves. Bring about 6 cups of water to a boil in a saucepan. Add the artichokes, and bring the water back to the boil. Cover, and boil over high heat for 20 minutes. Cool under cold running water.

ASPARAGUS IN MUSTARD SAUCE

Asparagus is a good source of folic acid and Vitamin B. I peel the stalks for this recipe (so they are completely edible) and cook the asparagus in just enough water so that most of it has evaporated by the time the asparagus is cooked, thus preserving the vitamins and nutrients in the vegetable. The pungent mustard dressing should be served at room temperature.

1¼ pounds asparagus (about 15 stalks)

¾ cup water

1 tablespoon Dijon-style mustard

2 tablespoons canola oil

¼ teaspoon freshly ground black pepper

½ teaspoon salt

1) Using a vegetable peeler, peel the asparagus stalks to remove the fibrous skin from the bottom third of the stalks. Cut the asparagus diagonally into 2 to 3 inch pieces. You should have about 3 cups.

2) Place the asparagus in a stainless steel saucepan and add the water. Cover, bring to a boil, and boil for 3 minutes, until the asparagus is just tender and most of the liquid has evaporated.

3) Drain off any remaining water and place asparagus in a bowl. Add the mustard, oil, pepper and salt, and mix well. Serve at room temperature.

Yield: 4 servings

BEANS & BROCCOLI DE RAPE

The cooked beans can be served warm with a little olive oil. Here, I have combined them with greens to enhance the flavor, lend color, and make them more nutritious. In addition to the fiber in the beans, the broccoli contains Vitamin A, present in all leafy green vegetables.

½ **pound white navy or Great Northern dried beans**

¾ **teaspoon salt**

2 **sprigs fresh thyme (or ½ tsp. dried thyme leaves)**

3 **ounces ham, cut into ½-inch dice**

1 **onion, peeled and cut into ¾-inch dice (1¼ cups)**

2 **tablespoons virgin olive oil**

2 **cloves garlic, peeled, crushed, and finely chopped**

¼ **teaspoon red pepper flakes**

½ **pound broccoli de rapé or Chinese broccoli, washed and cut into 2-inch pieces**

1) Wash the beans in cool water and remove and discard any pebbles or damaged beans.

2) In a pot, combine the beans with 4 cups cold water, salt, thyme, ham and onions. Bring to a boil, cover, reduce the heat and cook at a gentle boil for about 1½ hours, until the beans are tender and most of the water has been absorbed. There should be just enough water remaining so that the beans look moist and juicy.

3) Meanwhile, heat the oil in a skillet, add the garlic and pepper flakes, and sauté for about 10 seconds. Then add the broccoli de rapé (still wet from washing) and sauté for about 1 minute. Cover and cook over medium heat for 5 to 6 minutes, until the greens soften, become tender, and render some of their juices.

4) At serving time, combine beans and broccoli, rewarming them if necessary, and serve, if desired, with a little extra olive oil on each serving.

Yield: 4 servings

HOW TO COOK BEANS
It is a fallacy to believe that it takes a long time to cook dried beans. At the outset, there is no need to soak them beforehand, although you can do so for 1-2 hours if you like; longer soaking causes them to ferment, which makes them difficult to digest. I simply wash them, place them in a pot with cold water to cover, and cook them for 1 to 1½ hours, depending on the beans. Any type of little white beans–navy, Great Northern, pea, Boston–will work well here.

· FIRST COURSE ·

From top: Sautéed Eggplant Rolls and Sautéed Salmon on Greens.

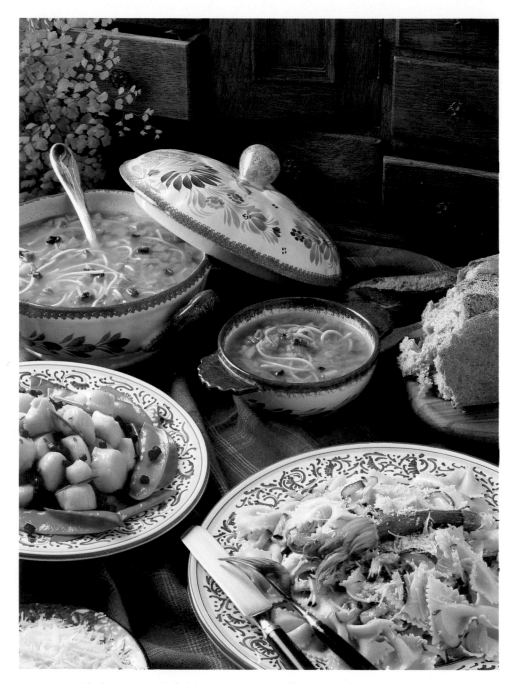

Clockwise: Potage de Légumes au Vermicelle; Pasta with Zucchini Sauce
and Sautéed Scallops with Snowpeas.

· FIRST COURSE ·

From left: Steamed Cod on Tapenade and Crab Cakes with Avocado Sauce.

· FIRST COURSE ·

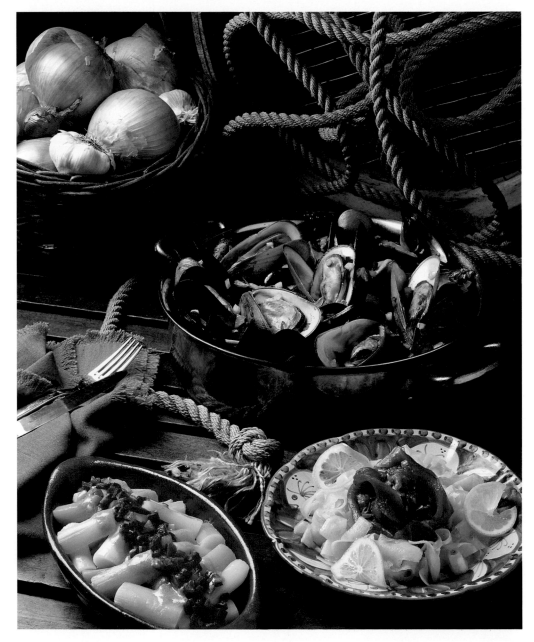

Clockwise: Moules Maison; Tuna Tartare on Marinated Cucumbers and Leeks with Tomato & Olive Oil.

LEEKS WITH TOMATO & OLIVE OIL

Fresh leeks, trimmed and cooked until just tender, are served with a tangy sauce flavored with diced tomatoes, olive oil and Dijon-style mustard. (Pictured on opposite page.)

4 medium to large leeks (about 1¼ lbs.), trimmed and washed

1 ripe tomato (about 7 oz.), peeled, seeded, and cut into ¼-inch pieces

3 tablespoons virgin olive oil

1 tablespoon red wine vinegar

1 tablespoon Dijon-style mustard

1 teaspoon Worcestershire sauce

½ teaspoon salt

¼ teaspoon freshly ground black pepper

1) In a stainless steel saucepan, bring 2 cups of water to a boil. Add the leeks, bring back to the boil and boil gently, covered, for 10 minutes or until tender.

2) Drain (reserving the juice for soup) and when cool enough to handle, squeeze the leeks to extract and reserve most of the remaining liquid.

3) Cut the leeks into 2-inch pieces and arrange the pieces in a gratin dish, mixing them to combine the white and green parts.

4) Mix together the tomato, oil, vinegar, mustard, Worcestershire sauce, salt and pepper, and spoon the mixture over the leeks. Serve lukewarm or at room temperature.

Yield: 4 servings

A WORD ABOUT LEEKS
Cook leeks in unsalted water; the resulting leek stock has a wonderfully intense flavor, making it ideal to keep, refrigerated or frozen, for use in soups. Use most of the green from the leeks, trimming off and discarding only the tips of the leaves and wilted or damaged outer leaves. Leaving them attached at the root end, cut the leeks open and wash them thoroughly.

STEAMED ENDIVES IN LEMON JUICE

Braised with lemon juice, steamed endives are a refreshing vegetable and they make a wonderful first course. Served lukewarm with this seasoned juice, they make a great accompaniment to meat and fish.

4   large or 8 small endives (¾ lb.)
1   tablespoon fresh lemon juice
3   l-inch strips of lemon peel, removed with a vegetable peeler and cut into 12 pieces
1   tablespoon unsalted butter
¼   cup water
½   teaspoon sugar
¼   teaspoon salt

1) Rinse the endives thoroughly and cut them in half lengthwise, if they are large, or leave them whole, if small.

2) Place the endives (preferably in one layer) in a stainless steel saucepan. Add the lemon juice, lemon peel, butter, water, sugar, and salt.

3) Bring to a boil, and place an inverted plate slightly smaller than the pan over the endives. Cover the pan with a lid, reduce the heat to low, and cook the endives for 20 minutes, until just tender. Serve lukewarm.

Yield: 4 servings

A SPECIAL TECHNIQUE
In this recipe, I cook the endives with a little lemon juice, lemon peel, butter, water, sugar, and salt. You will notice that there is only a little liquid in the bottom of the pan when you begin the cooking process. If a plate is placed on top of the endives, however, to press down on them as cook, they will render a lot of juice, and, in fact, eventually finish cooking almost immersed in their own cooking liquid.

SAUTEED EGGPLANT ROLLS

This is a great party dish, perfect on a buffet table. The eggplant can be sautéed and stuffed ahead and the filling mixture changed at will to accommodate leftover meat or fish. The vinaigrette tomatoes, delicious with the eggplant, are also good with poached fish or mixed with a green salad. (Pictured on page 35.)

¼ cup canola oil

1 eggplant (1 lb.), cut into 16 slices, each about ⅜-inch thick

Salt and freshly ground black pepper to taste

3 tablespoons olive oil

1 small onion (3 oz.), chopped

3 ounces mushrooms, chopped

2 to 3 large cloves garlic, peeled, crushed and finely chopped

4 ounces Monterey Jack or Beaumont cheese, coarsely chopped or grated

3 tablespoons golden raisins

1 tablespoon Worcestershire sauce

½ teaspoon salt

½ teaspoon freshly ground black pepper

4 tablespoons chopped chives

Vinaigrette Tomatoes

2 large ripe tomatoes (1 lb.)

1 small onion (about 3 oz.), chopped (about ⅔ cup)

2 teaspoons red wine vinegar

2 tablespoons virgin olive oil

½ teaspoon salt

¼ teaspoon freshly ground black pepper

1) Heat 2 tablespoons of the canola oil in a non-stick skillet and, when hot, add 8 slices of the eggplant. Sprinkle lightly with salt and pepper, and cook 5 minutes on each side over medium heat. Remove to a dish and repeat with the remaining eggplant. Set aside.

2) Heat 2 tablespoons of the olive oil in a skillet and sauté the onion in the hot oil for 1 minute. Add the mushrooms and sauté for another minute. Stir in the garlic and remove from the heat.

3) In a bowl, combine the cheese with the onion-mushroom mixture and mix in the raisins, Worcestershire, salt, pepper, 3 tablespoons of chives, and the remaining tablespoon of olive oil. Divide the mixture between the 16 slices of eggplant and roll to form stuffed eggplant rolls.

For vinaigrette tomatoes:

1) Cut the tomatoes in half horizontally and gently squeeze out the seeds. Chop into ¼-inch pieces.

2) In a bowl, combine the chopped tomatoes, onions, vinegar, oil, salt, and pepper.

3) To serve, spread the tomato mixture on a large serving plate and arrange the eggplant rolls on top. Sprinkle with the remaining tablespoon of chives and serve at room temperature with some of the tomato mixture.

Yield: 4 servings

GRATIN OF SCALLIONS

These scallions can be cooked and coated with the finishing half-and-half and bread crumbs ahead, ready for reheating at the last minute. If you prepare them early and allow them to cool, however, increase the baking time by 5 minutes to ensure that they are hot.

4   bunches of scallions (1¼ lbs.), about 6 scallions to the bunch

1   cup water

½   cup half-and-half

½   slice fresh bread

2   tablespoons grated Parmesan cheese

¼   teaspoon salt

¼   teaspoon freshly ground black pepper

1) Remove and discard the top 2 inches and any damaged or wilted leaves from the scallions. Rinse them thoroughly.

2) Place the scallions in a stainless steel saucepan with the water. Bring to a boil, cover and cook over high heat for 5 minutes. Most of the liquid will have evaporated.

3) Arrange the scallions in a gratin dish and pour the half-and-half over them. Break the bread into pieces, place in the bowl of a food processor, and process them momentarily, just until crumbed. (You should have ¼ cup.)

4) In a small bowl, mix together the bread crumbs, cheese, salt, and pepper, and sprinkle the mixture over the scallions. Bake in a preheated 450° oven for 10 minutes.

Yield: 4 servings

PASTA & ZUCCHINI

I make this extra simple pasta sauce with zucchini, garlic, salt, pepper and olive oil. The combination of vegetables and cooking liquid creates a rich, satisfying, colorful pasta sauce that is not too caloric. (Pictured on page 36.)

6	ounces (2 rounded cups) farfalle (bow-tie shaped) pasta
2	small zucchini (9 oz.)
3	tablespoons virgin olive oil
8	cloves garlic, peeled and sliced (about 2 tbs.)
½	teaspoon salt
¼	teaspoon freshly ground black pepper
2	tablespoons grated Parmesan cheese

1) Bring 10 cups of water to a boil in a large saucepan. Add the farfalle and cook over high heat for 13 to 15 minutes, until done as desired.

2) Meanwhile, wash the zucchini and cut them in half lengthwise and then into ¼-inch slices. Then, stack up the slices and cut them into ¼-inch sticks. You should have 2 cups.

3) Heat the olive oil in a skillet . When hot, sauté the zucchini sticks over high heat for 4 minutes, until lightly browned and cooked through. Add the garlic and sauté for 30 seconds longer.

4) When the pasta is cooked, remove ⅓ cup of the cooking liquid and place it in a bowl large enough to hold the pasta. Drain the pasta through a colander and add it to the bowl. Add the zucchini, salt, and pepper, and toss to combine. Serve with the grated cheese.

Yield: 4 servings

PASTA WITH FRESH VEGETABLE SAUCE

Here's a low-calorie pasta dish than can be made in less than 20 minutes. Remember to put the pasta cooking water on to boil before you begin this recipe; it only takes about 7 minutes to make the sauce and about the same amount of time to cook the pasta, so bringing the water to a boil is the most time-consuming part of this preparation.

½ pound spaghetti (#4)

¼ cup virgin olive oil

1 large red onion, peeled and sliced thin (1½ cups)

1 small eggplant (6 oz.), cut into ½-inch pieces

3 to 4 cloves garlic, peeled, crushed and finely chopped

2 ripe tomatoes (12 oz.), seeded and cut into ½-inch pieces

1 teaspoon salt

½ teaspoon freshly ground black pepper

2 tablespoons coarsely chopped parsley

About 2 tablespoons grated Parmesan cheese

1) Bring 3 quarts of water to the boil. Add the pasta, return the water to the boil and cook for about 8 minutes, until the pasta is just tender to the bite.

2) Meanwhile, heat the olive oil in a large saucepan and sauté the onions and eggplant until soft and lightly browned, 6 to 7 minutes. Remove the pan from the heat and mix in the garlic. Add the tomatoes, salt, and pepper; mix thoroughly and set aside.

3) Remove ⅓ cup of pasta cooking liquid and add it to the eggplant mixture. Drain the pasta, add it to the saucepan and toss to coat it with the vegetables.

4) Divide among four plates, sprinkle with the parsley, and serve with cheese to taste.

Yield: 4 servings

PREVENTING STICKY PASTA
Notice that I don't salt the pasta cooking water. I see no difference in the cooking process, and I'd rather save the salt for use in the sauce. To prevent the cooked pasta from sticking together or being too dense, I reserve a little of the pasta cooking water and add it to the vegetables before tossing them with the pasta.

MUSHROOM-STUFFED POTATO PANCAKES

Potato pancakes-conventionally deep-fried-are often as many as 500 calories each. Sautéed simply in a little oil in a non-stick skillet, as they are here, they amount to about 200 calories for each portion. I serve them as a first course but they make a delightful main course, too.

4   to 5 potatoes (about 1½ lbs.), cleaned

¾   teaspoon salt

½   teaspoon freshly ground black pepper

5   tablespoons canola oil

4   shallots, peeled and sliced (⅓ cup)

2   cloves garlic, peeled, crushed and finely chopped (l tsp.)

4   ounces mushrooms, chopped (1¼ cups)

12   oil-cured black olives, pitted and cut into ½-inch dice

1) Place the potatoes in a saucepan and cover with cool water. Bring to a boil, and cook gently for 30 minutes or until tender. Remove and let the potatoes cool. Then peel and push through a food mill. Season with ½ teaspoon of salt and ¼ teaspoon of pepper.

2) Meanwhile, in a large skillet or saucepan heat 1 tablespoon of oil, add shallots and sauté for one minute. Add garlic and mushrooms, and cook for about 3 minutes, until the moisture is almost gone. Remove from the heat and add the olives and remaining salt and pepper. Cool.

3) Divide the cold potato pureé into 24 equal-size balls. Arrange the balls about 6 inches apart on a large sheet of plastic wrap. Cover with a second piece of plastic and press on each ball to create a pancake about 3 inches in diameter and ¼-inch thick. Spoon 1 tablespoon of the mixture on 12 pancakes; cover with the remaining pancakes.

4) Heat the remaining 4 tablespoons of oil in two large non-stick skillets over medium to high heat. When hot, add the filled pancakes in a single layer and cook them for about 3 minutes. Turn carefully with a large spatula and cook for about 3 minutes on the other side. Remove to a serving platter and serve immediately or set aside and reheat in the oven or under the broiler, just before serving.

Yield: 6 servings

POTATO CREPES WITH CAVIAR

These crepes, made from a batter that contains just 2 whole eggs plus 1 egg white, are served covered with caviar, the amount adjusted to suit your pocketbook. The two best types of red caviar are "natural" and "red." I've used a good, moderately expensive natural red caviar. Then, to make the dish superlative, a little of the expensive black caviar from sturgeon–Beluga, Osetra, or Sevruga–is placed in the center of each crepe.

Crepes

1   large potato (about 9 oz.)

2   large whole eggs plus 1 egg white

⅓   cup milk

¼   teaspoon salt

⅛   teaspoon Tabasco sauce

2   tablespoons flour

4   tablespoons canola oil

Garnishes

About 8 ounces natural red salmon caviar (about 12 tbs.)

1   cup sour cream

1   tablespoon finely chopped chives

About 2 ounces (3 tbs.) Beluga, Osetra, or Sevruga caviar (Look for "Malossol", which means lightly salted)

For crepes:

1) Place the potato in a saucepan with water to cover and bring to a boil. Cover, reduce the heat, and boil gently for 30 minutes, until the potato is tender. Drain, peel, and press through a food mill into a bowl.

2) Add the whole eggs and egg white and mix well with a whisk. Then mix in the milk, salt and Tabasco sauce.

3) In a skillet, heat 2 teaspoons of oil. When hot, add about ¼ cup of the crepe mixture, which should spread to create a circle about 4½ to 5-inches in diameter. Cook over medium heat for about 2 minutes on each side.

4) Transfer to a cookie sheet and set aside in a warm oven while you make five more crepes with the remaining batter and oil.

For garnishes:

1) To serve, spread the entire top surface of the lukewarm crepes with red caviar, extending it clear to the edge of each crepe. Mound 2 tablespoons of sour cream in the center of each crepe, and sprinkle it with chives. Finally, place about 1½ teaspoons of black caviar in the center of the sour cream mound. Serve immediately.

Yield: 4 servings

CRAB CAKES WITH AVOCADO SAUCE

Although I use real crabmeat for my crabmeat cakes, you can substitute *surimi*, the product of an old Japanese procedure that involves making crabmeat with protein and less exotic fish like pollack and cod. This imitation crabmeat is widely available in markets and would be good prepared like this. Be sure to add the bread crumbs at the end of the mixing process and to toss them very lightly. (Pictured on page 37.)

Crab Cakes

8	ounces crabmeat
¼	teaspoon freshly ground black pepper
¼	teaspoon dried thyme
1	tablespoon chives
⅛	teaspoon Tabasco sauce
¼	teaspoon salt
3	tablespoons mayonnaise
1½	slices bread, processed to make ¾-cup crumbs
2	tablespoons peanut oil

Avocado Sauce

1	ripe tomato (5 oz.)
1	small ripe avocado (6 oz.)
1	tablespoon red wine vinegar
2	tablespoons peanut oil
¼	teaspoon freshly ground black pepper
¼	teaspoon salt
3	tablespoons water
1	tablespoon chopped chives, for garnish

For crab cakes:

1) Cut the crabmeat into ¼ inch pieces. (You should have 1½ lightly packed cups.)

2) In a bowl, mix the crabmeat with the pepper, thyme, chives, Tabasco, salt and mayonnaise. Add the bread crumbs and toss them lightly into the mixture. Divide the mixture and form it into four patties, each about 1-inch thick and weighing about ½ ounce. Handle the mixture gently; it should barely hold together.

3) In a large skillet, heat the oil. When hot, place the patties carefully in the skillet and sauté them gently in the oil over medium heat for 3 to 4 minutes on each side.

For avocado sauce:

1) While the crabmeat cakes are cooking, skin, seed, and coarsely chop the tomato. Peel and pit the avocado and coarsely chop it. Place the chopped tomatoes and avocado in a bowl and add the vinegar, peanut oil, pepper, salt and water.

2) To serve, spoon some sauce onto four individual plates, sprinkle with chives and place a patty on top. Serve immediately.

Yield: 4 servings

CLAM CROQUETTES

I serve these clam croquettes on salad greens, which absorb some of their richness and help balance the dish. You can substitute pieces of oyster or raw shrimp for the clams in this recipe. There are just enough bread crumbs and mayonnaise to bind the mixture together so that it can be formed into patties and sautéed. Use a low-calorie mayonnaise to eliminate a few additional calories.

1	tablespoon virgin olive oil
1	small onion (about 2 oz.), chopped (¼ cup)
2	scallions, minced (about ¼ cup)
8	ounces shelled fresh clams, drained and cut into ¼-inch pieces
½	teaspoon chopped Jalapeño pepper
2	tablespoons mayonnaise
¼	teaspoon Tabasco sauce
¼	teaspoon salt
3	slices white bread
3	tablespoons safflower oil

Seasoned Salad

1½	cups mixture of salad greens, washed and thoroughly dried
1	tablespoon peanut oil
1	teaspoon red wine vinegar
⅛	teaspoon salt
⅛	teaspoon freshly ground black pepper

For croquettes:

1) Heat the olive oil in a skillet. When hot, add the onions and scallions, and sauté for 1 minute.

2) Remove from the heat and place in a bowl. Stir in the clams, Jalapeño pepper, mayonnaise, Tabasco and salt, and mix well.

3) Break the bread slices into pieces and place them in the bowl of a food processor. Process briefly, just until crumbed. You should have about 1½ cups of fresh bread crumbs. Add the crumbs to the mixture in the bowl and toss them in lightly. Form the mixture into twelve patties.

4) Heat half the oil in a skillet. When hot, add six patties and sauté for 2½ minutes on each side. Repeat with the remainder of the oil and patties.

For seasoned salad:

1) In a bowl, toss the salad greens with the oil, vinegar, salt, and pepper.

2) Arrange the greens on four individual plates and top each serving with 3 croquettes. Serve.

Yield: 4 servings

· FIRST COURSE ·

SMOKED WHITEFISH MOLD

This is an ideal party dish because it can and should be made ahead. After lining the molds with plastic wrap, the layers of filling are added. The compacted mixture can be removed immediately from the molds and stored until serving time in the plastic wrap. You'll need to buy about 10 ounces of whole fish to get 5 ounces of flesh.

4   teaspoons chopped chives

6   tablespoons cream cheese

4   large radishes, cut into thin slices

5   ounces completely boned, skinned, smoked whitefish or chub

⅛   teaspoon freshly ground black pepper

4   slices bread, toasted and cut into triangles

1) Line four ½-cup molds with plastic wrap. Place 1 teaspoon of chives and 2 teaspoons of cream cheese in the bottom of each mold, pressing on the cheese to imbed the chives.

2) Arrange about 3 slices of radish on top of the cheese in each cup and press down again to make the mixture more compact. Place about ⅛ of the fish (1½ tablespoons) on top of each and add another 2 teaspoons of cream cheese. Sprinkle with the pepper, and add another layer of fish and a layer of radish.

3) Cover with plastic wrap and press on the mixture to make it more compact. Refrigerate until serving time.

4) To serve, unmold, remove the plastic wrap and serve with toast triangles.

Yield: 4 servings

VARIATIONS
In this recipe, I use smoked whitefish, although smoked salmon or another type of smoked fish can be substituted. In place of the radishes, you can layer cucumbers or other vegetables in the molds; caviar, arranged between layers of cream cheese, is even a possibility here. If you're counting calories, the cream cheese can be replaced with cottage cheese.

STEAMED COD ON TAPENADE

Tapanade comes from the word *tapeno*, which means "capers" in Provencal, where this concoction originated. I add a coarsely chopped fig to my version, which gives it an interesting taste of sweetness. The steamed cod (or another variety of fish, if you prefer) is placed directly on the strongly flavored tapenade. (Pictured on page 37.)

Tapenade

⅔ cup black oil-cured olives, pitted and chopped fine

8 anchovy fillets in oil, drained, and chopped fine

2 tablespoons capers, drained, rinsed under cool tap water and chopped fine

2 small black dried figs, chopped fine (3 tbs.)

4 tablespoons virgin olive oil

¼ teaspoon freshly ground black pepper

2 tablespoons water

¼ pound thick cod fillets (4 pieces, 5 oz. each)

6 basil leaves, for garnish
A piece of tomato skin, cut into strips, for garnish

For tapenade:
1) In a bowl mix together the olives, anchovies, capers, figs, olive oil, and pepper. Set aside.

For cod:
1) Place about 1-inch of water in a steamer and bring it to a strong boil. Arrange the fish in a single layer on a plate, and place the plate in the steamer. Steam the fish, covered, for 4 to 5 minutes.

2) Meanwhile, arrange the tapenade mixture on individual plates. When the fish pieces are cooked, place one in the center of each plate. Sprinkle with the basil and tomato skin strips, and serve.

3) Thinly slice the basil leaves to make a chiffonade and sprinkle over the cod. Arrange the tomato strips on top and serve.

Yield: 4 servings

STEAMING TECHNIQUE
I steam the fish in a conventional steamer, but, if you don't have one, place it in a stainless steel pan containing approximately ½ inch of water and cook it, covered, for about 2 minutes on each side. By the time the fish has finished cooking, most of the water will have evaporated and the fish will, in a sense, be steamed.

· FIRST COURSE ·

SAUTEED SALMON ON GREENS

Salmon is a great seafood choice because it is available practically year round from your fish-monger. High in *omega 3*, salmon is recommended by doctors and is especially versatile, accommodating itself to poaching, braising, sautéeing, and grilling. (Pictured on page 35.)

4   skinless, boneless salmon fillet steaks (about 5 oz. each)

4   tablespoons virgin olive oil

½   pound spinach, thoroughly cleaned

¾   teaspoon salt

¼   teaspoon freshly ground black pepper

½   cup chopped onion

3   ripe tomatoes (about 1¼ lbs.), peeled, seeded and cut into ½-inch pieces

1   tablespoon coarsely chopped flat-leaf parsley

1) Arrange the salmon steaks on a plate, spoon 1 tablespoon olive oil over them, cover with plastic wrap and refrigerate.

2) In a skillet, heat 1 tablespoon of the remaining olive oil. When hot, sauté the spinach for 1½ minutes. Mix in ¼ teaspoon of the salt and ⅛ teaspoon of the pepper, and divide the spinach among four plates.

3) Heat the remaining 2 tablespoons of olive oil in the skillet and sauté the onion for 1 minute. Add the tomatoes, ¼ teaspoon of the salt, and ⅛ teaspoon of the pepper, and cook for about 30 seconds. Set aside.

4) Remove the salmon from the refrigerator, and sprinkle it with the remaining ¼ teaspoon salt. Heat a non-stick skillet until very hot, add the salmon steaks, and sauté for 1½ minutes on each side. Let rest in the pan a few minutes before serving.

5) Spoon some of the onion-tomato mixture over the spinach and top with salmon. Sprinkle with parsley and serve immediately.

Yield: 4 servings

SPECIAL TECHNIQUES
Notice that the steaks are macerated in a little olive oil; that light coating of fat is all that is required to cook them, which only takes a couple of minutes in a very hot skillet. The spinach is cooked "dry," the only moisture being the small amount of water clinging to the leaves after the vegetable is washed; this helps retain nutrients, color, and vitamins. And the tomatoes are also lightly sautéed so they keep their fresh, sweet taste.

TUNA TARTARE ON MARINATED CUCUMBERS

The tartare is served on a fresh-tasting garnish composed of sliced cucumber, vinegar, minced chives, peanut oil, and salt. Delicious and attractive, this simple but sophisticated dish makes a great first course. The tuna should be chopped by hand rather than in a food processor. (Pictured on page 38.)

1   **pound completely cleaned raw tuna**

1   **large shallot, peeled and finely chopped (2 tbs.)**

2   **cloves garlic, peeled, crushed, and finely chopped (1 tsp.)**

1   **teaspoon salt**

½   **teaspoon freshly ground black pepper**

2   **tablespoons virgin olive oil**

1½ **teaspoons white vinegar**

¼   **teaspoon Tabasco sauce**

Cucumber Garnish

1   **cucumber (about 12 oz.)**

1   **teaspoon vinegar**

1   **teaspoon peanut oil**

¼   **teaspoon salt**

3   **tablespoons minced chives, for garnish**

TUNA TARTARE
Tuna tartare is a modern recipe inspired by Japanese *sashimi*. Use only super-fresh fish purchased from a reputable fishmonger, and if you are afraid of any type of parasites, request that your fish-monger freeze the fish you buy for a minimum of 5 to 7 days at 0 degrees or less, a bit colder than most home freezers can be set.

1) Reserve four small slices (1 oz. each) of the tuna and chop the remainder by hand into a ¼-inch dice. Place one of the reserved slices of tuna between two sheets of plastic wrap, and pound it into a thin round about 4 inches in diameter. Repeat with the other three slices.

2) Remove the top sheet of plastic wrap from the slices, and season them lightly with salt. Set aside.

3) In a bowl mix the chopped tuna with the shallots, garlic, salt, pepper, olive oil, vinegar, and Tabasco. (Mixed with vinegar, the chopped tuna will "whiten" somewhat, becoming opaque. This is because the acidic acid in the vinegar coagulates, thus "cooking" the protein in the tuna.)

For cucumber garnish:
1) Peel the cucumber and cut long, thin strips from it with a vegetable peeler on all sides until you come to the seeds. Discard the seeds, and mix the strips with the vinegar, oil, and salt.

2) To serve, divide the garnish among four plates. Form the chopped tuna mixture into 4 balls and place one on top of the cucumbers on each of the plates. Wrap a slice of tuna around each tuna ball, sprinkle with the chives, and serve.

Yield: 4 servings

TROUT SAUTE TERRY

Fresh farm-raised trout are available all over the country now. Delicately flavored, they can often be purchased live from a tank at the local supermarket, so you are guaranteed of their freshness. I created a sauce adding mushrooms, tomatoes, olive pieces and diced lemon to the pan drippings. The result is not only delicious, but beautiful to look at.

2   tablespoons unsalted butter

2   tablespoons canola oil

4   fresh eviscerated trout (about 12 oz. each)

½   teaspoon salt

½   teaspoon freshly ground black pepper

1½ cups diced mushrooms (3 or 4 large mushrooms)

1   large tomato (8 oz.), halved, seeded and cut into ½-inch pieces

24 oil-cured olives, pitted and cut into ⅜-inch dice

1   small lemon, peeled and cut into ⅜-inch dice (¼ cup)

2   tablespoons chopped chives

1) Heat the butter and oil in one very large or two 9-inch non-stick skillets. Pat the trout dry and place them in the hot butter. Sprinkle with the salt and pepper and cook over medium to high heat, covered, for 4 minutes. Then turn and cook on the other side for 4 minutes.

2) Transfer the trout to a platter, and set it aside in a warm place. The trout can be served with the bone in and head left on, or it can be be boned and returned to the serving platter before being carried to the dining room.

3) To the drippings in the pan, add the mushrooms. Sauté for 1 minute, then add the diced tomatoes and sauté for 1 minute longer. Add the olive pieces and the diced lemon, and toss well. Spoon the contents of the pan over the trout and serve.

Yield: 4 servings

SAUTEED SCALLOPS WITH SNOW PEAS

This red, green and white-colored dish is perfect for the holidays, and can be served as a first course. Ready in a few minutes, the snow peas are cooked in a minimum of water and the scallops require only brief sautéeing at the last moment. (Pictured on page 36.)

½ pound snow peas, trimmed

¼ cup water

½ red bell pepper (4 oz.)

1 tablespoon unsalted butter

2 tablespoons virgin olive oil

¾ pound (12 oz.) small sea scallops

¼ teaspoon salt

¼ teaspoon freshly ground black pepper

½ teaspoon Tabasco sauce

1) Place the snow peas in one very large or two smaller skillets with the water. Cook, covered, for 2 minutes, and then uncover and cook until dry.

2) Meanwhile, remove the skin from the bell pepper with a vegetable peeler and cut the flesh into ¼-inch dice. Add the red pepper to the snow peas and half the butter and oil. Sauté over high heat for 2 minutes. Arrange on individual plates.

3) Sprinkle the scallops with the salt and pepper, and heat the remaining butter and oil in a skillet. When very hot, add the scallops and the Tabasco sauce, and sauté over very high heat for 2 to 3 minutes.

4) Arrange the scallops on the snow peas and serve immediately.

Yield: 4 servings

NUTRITIONAL INFORMATION
The snow peas are cooked very quickly–just until the water evaporates–so that all the nutrients are left behind. The peas are low in calories and high in fiber and Vitamin A, and the red pepper, also low in calories, is high in Vitamin C.

· FIRST COURSE ·

HOT SHRIMP ON SPINACH

The shrimp are shelled in this recipe, but I often make this dish at home with unshelled shrimp, which the family peels right at the table. For guests, it is better to buy the shrimp shelled or to shell them yourself. They only take a few minutes to cook this way and are easier to eat. Remember to cook the greens first. (Pictured on page 1.)

1   pound large shrimp (about 16), unshelled

½   teaspoon dried thyme

½   teaspoon dried oregano

1   teaspoon dried tarragon

¼   teaspoon dried ground coriander

¼   teaspoon freshly ground black pepper

⅛   teaspoon cayenne pepper

2   tablespoons virgin olive oil

Greens

2   tablespoons virgin olive oil

10   ounces cleaned spinach

¼   teaspoon salt

¼   teaspoon freshly ground black pepper

1) Shell the shrimp and sprinkle them with the thyme, oregano, tarragon, coriander, and peppers. Place them in a single layer in a dish and sprinkle with the oil. Set aside.

For greens:
1) In a saucepan, heat 2 tablespoons olive oil. When hot, sauté the spinach for 2 minutes. Add the salt and pepper and combine. Divide among four plates.

2) Heat an aluminum or black iron skillet until very, very hot. Place the oiled shrimp in one layer in the skillet, and cook over high heat for 1 minute. Turn and cook for 1½ minutes on the other side.

3) To serve, place 4 shrimp on top of the greens on each plate. Add 2 tablespoons of water to the juices in the pan and mix to deglaze. Pour the juices over the shrimp and serve.

Yield: 4 servings

MUSSELS GRATINEE

These mussels are excellent as a first course. They can be opened up to a day ahead, the seasonings arranged on top, and then the dish refrigerated until ready to place under the broiler. The juices released by the mussels can be frozen for use in soups or sauces. (Pictured on page 38.)

24   mussels (about 2 lbs.)
3   cloves garlic, peeled
½   cup loose flat-leaf parsley
2   slices white bread
⅛   teaspoon salt
¼   teaspoon freshly ground black pepper
2   tablespoons virgin olive oil
     A few drops of Tabasco sauce (optional)

1) To open the mussels, place them in a pot without any liquid or seasonings and cook over high heat, covered, for 6 to 8 minutes, just until they have opened and released their juice. (Do not overcook because they will be re-cooked under the broiler at serving time.)

2) Remove and discard the empty shell of each cooked mussel and arrange the mussels in the half shells on a cookie sheet.

3) Place garlic and parsley in the bowl of a food processor and process until coarsely chopped. Add the 2 slices of bread and process until the mixture is finely chopped and fluffy.

4) Transfer the parsley-bread mixture to a mixing bowl and add the salt, pepper, olive oil, and, if desired, Tabasco. Mix the ingredients lightly with your fingers or a fork, tossing them gently so they are moistened with the oil but still fluffy. Sprinkle the mixture over the mussels.

5) At serving time, place the mussels under the broiler for 2 to 3 minutes, until nicely browned on top and warm inside.

Yield: 4 servings

BEEF CARPACCIO

In my version of carpaccio, I eliminate the traditional mayonnaise accompaniment and serve the beef with a little olive oil, black pepper, red onion, basil leaves, and Parmesan cheese. Quick and easy to prepare, it is delicious and attractive.

1	12-ounce piece beef shell (also called New York strip), sinew and fat removed
½	teaspoon salt
½	teaspoon freshly ground black pepper
1	small red onion or piece of red onion (2 oz.), sliced very thin
10	large basil leaves, shredded into thin strips
1½	ounces Parmesan cheese (in a chunk)
4	tablespoons extra virgin olive oil

1) Clean any remaining fat from the exterior of the meat (you should have 8 to 9 oz.) and cut it into four pieces, each about 2 ounces.

2) Butterfly each piece and pound it between two pieces of plastic wrap until it is quite thin and about 7 to 8 inches in diameter. Arrange a piece on each of four plates and sprinkle it with the salt and pepper.

3) Place the onion slices in a strainer and rinse under cold water. Pat dry and distribute over the meat; sprinkle the shredded basil on top.

4) Using a vegetable peeler, cut shavings of the cheese and let them drop directly on top of the meat. Sprinkle 1 tablespoon of oil on each portion and serve immediately.

Yield: 4 servings

A WORD ABOUT CARPACCIO
Vittore Carpaccio was a 15th century Venetian painter who favored red and white on his canvasses. When the creators of this dish featuring thinly pounded raw beef–bright red, of course–decided to serve it with a strip of mayonnaise, it seemed appropriate to name it after the painter most associated with these two colors.

· MAIN COURSE ·

Moules Maison
Red Snapper in Potato Jackets
Salmon Pojarski
Couscous of Lobster
Catfish on Ratatouille
Chicken & Seafood Paella
Chicken Legs with Wine & Yams
Chicken in Tarragon Sauce
Grilled Chicken with Cabbage Anchoyade
Poule au Pot
Poulet au Vin Rouge
Brown Rice Chicken Fricassee
Grilled Quail on Quinoa with Sunflower Seeds
Roasted Turkey with Mushroom Stuffing
Ragout of Rabbit
Veal Chops with Mushrooms
Veal Roast with Artichokes
Wine Merchant Steak
Spicy Beef Shell Roast
Grilled Savory Lamb Chops
Irish Lamb Stew
Grilled Leg of Lamb
Saucisses au Chou on Lentils
Braised Pork Cocotte
Smoked Pork Roast with Mustard-Honey Glaze

MOULES MAISON

This is the simplest way to cook mussels–all the ingredients are combined in a saucepan and the mixture is cooked together for a few minutes. There is enough juice in the mussels, mushrooms and tomatoes to create a nice sauce. Serve this dish for casual dining or as a first course as pictured on page 38.

4	**pounds mussels, cleaned**
6	**plum tomatoes (1 lb.), seeded and cut into 1½-inch cubes (about 2½ cups)**
6	**scallions, trimmed and cut into ¼-inch dice**
½	**pound mushrooms, cut into ½-inch dice (about 2½ cups)**
2	**onions (8 oz.), peeled and coarsely chopped (2 cups)**
8	**cloves garlic, peeled and sliced (2 tbs.)**
1	**cup dry white wine**
4	**tablespoons virgin olive oil**
1½	**teaspoons Tabasco sauce**
½	**teaspoon salt or to taste**
¼	**cup coarsely chopped flat-leaf parsley**

1) Place the mussels, tomatoes, scallions, mushrooms, onions, garlic, wine, olive oil, Tabasco and salt in a large saucepan and bring to a boil. Cover and cook 6 to 7 minutes, stirring occasionally, until all the mussels have opened. (Remove and discard any that fail to open.)

2) Divide the mussels among four dishes and either serve as is, or remove and discard the shell halves without meat and serve the mussels in the half shell. Spoon sauce over the mussels, sprinkle them with parsley, and serve with French fries (page 107).

Yield: 4 servings

· MAIN COURSE ·

RED SNAPPER IN POTATO JACKETS

Cooked between layers of sliced potato, these moist fish fillets make an impressive main course. The zucchini garnish makes a good first course, too. Serve just as they emerge from the skillet, while the potatoes are still crisp. (Pictured on page 71.)

2	large potatoes (1 lb.)
4	1-inch thick fish fillets (5 oz. each) from red snapper, black fish, or sea bass
¼	teaspoon salt
⅛	teaspoon freshly ground black pepper

Zucchini Garnish

1	medium zucchini (about 8 oz.)
1	tablespoon peanut oil
1	tablespoon soy sauce
2	tablespoons virgin olive oil
2	tablespoons peanut oil
2	tablespoons chopped parsley

VARIATIONS
Any variety of thick fish fillet will work here. If you can't get a sea water fish like snapper, use trout, perch, or catfish fillets instead, altering the cooking time to accommodate variations in thickness. Obviously, the most important consideration when selecting the fish is freshness.

USING A MANDOLINE
* I use a mandoline, a professional slicer made of stainless steel, but any slicer (including the 1 mm blade on a food processor) will work well.

1) Peel the potatoes and thinly slice them lengthwise.* (You should have about 50 slices.) Wash potatoes, drain off water, and pat slices dry with paper towels.

2) Place 4 pieces of plastic wrap (each 6 inches square) on the table. Arrange 6 overlapping slices of potato in the center of each square and place a piece of fish on top. Sprinkle with the salt and pepper. Arrange another 6 slices of potato, also overlapping, on top of the fish and fold the plastic around them so they are completely wrapped. Refrigerate until ready to cook (not too far ahead, or the potatoes will discolor), or cook immediately.

3) Cut the zucchini into 2-inch chunks, then into ⅛-inch slices, and, finally, into a julienne (yielding about 3 cups). Spread the zucchini out on a tray and place in a preheated 400° oven for 5 to 6 minutes to soften it. Transfer the zucchini to a bowl and toss it with the 1 tablespoon of peanut oil and soy sauce.

4) At cooking time, divide the 2 tablespoons each of olive oil and peanut oil between 2 non-stick skillets and place over medium heat. Carefully unwrap the potato-fish packages and, with a large spatula, transfer them to the skillets, placing two in each skillet. Sauté 5 minutes, then carefully turn (so the arrangement is not disturbed), and sauté for 5 minutes or until potatoes are nicely browned.

5) To serve, arrange the zucchini in a circle to border the plate and place the fish in potato jackets in the center. Sprinkle with parsley and serve.

Yield: 4 servings

· MAIN COURSE ·

SALMON POJARSKI

Pojarski of salmon used to be made with a puree of salmon, egg yolks, bread, and cream. In my updated recipe, the salmon is coarsely chopped, yielding a better texture, and is held together with a little bread and an egg white. Instead of moistening the bread with cream (doing a *panade*), I use chicken stock and other seasonings, and add raw mushrooms, which give moisture and taste to

Crudite Sauce

½	cucumber, peeled, seeded and finely chopped (½ cup)
⅓	red bell pepper
2	scallions
1	clove garlic, peeled, crushed and finely chopped
2	tablespoons vinegar
⅓	cup water
1	teaspoon sugar
½	teaspoon salt
⅛	teaspoon freshly ground black pepper
⅛	teaspoon Tabasco sauce

For sauce:

1) Peel the cucumber, remove the seeds and chop finely, to make about ½ cup. Place in a large bowl.

2) Using a vegetable peeler, remove the skin from the bell pepper and finely chop the flesh, to make ¼ cup. Add to the cucumbers.

3) Mince the scallions finely and add to the bowl along with the garlic, vinegar, water, sugar salt, pepper and Tabasco. Set aside until ready to serve.

SALMON
Salmon is one of the fatty fish recommended by doctors; it tends to lower fat in the blood and reduce triglycerides. Potatoes, a complex carbohydrate high in potassium, contain only 20 calories per ounce, while broccoli is loaded with Vitamins C and A, potassium and iron. The refreshing poached orange desert contains Vitamin C.

· MAIN COURSE ·

the patties. Don't add the mushrooms more than a few hours ahead, however, as they tend to bleed and discolor the mixture. The salmon is served with a refreshing crudite sauce that is also good with grilled poultry or meat.

Patties

1	medium onion (4 oz.)
2	ounces mushrooms
1	tablespoon canola oil
3	tablespoons water
2	slices (2 oz.) white bread
⅓	cup chicken stock, preferably home-made (see Chicken Broth, page 30)
1	pound salmon, cleaned of skin, sinew and bones (14 oz. trimmed)
1	egg white
2	tablespoons coarsely chopped parsley
2	tablespoons chopped chives
½	teaspoon salt
¼	teaspoon freshly ground black pepper

For salmon patties:

1) Coarsely chop the onions and mushrooms. You should have 1 cup of each. Combine the onions, oil, and water in a skillet, and bring the mixture to a boil. Cook, covered, for 1 minute. Uncover, and add the mushrooms. Cook until most of the moisture has evaporated and the onions and mushrooms are beginning to fry. Cool.

2) Place the bread in a food processor, and process to make 1 cup bread crumbs. Transfer to a bowl, and mix in the stock.

3) Coarsely chop the salmon, cutting it into ¼-inch pieces. Add the salmon along with the cooked onions and mushrooms, egg white, parsley, chives, salt and pepper. Mix until well combined. Divide the mixture into four equal parts, each about 6 oz. and form into round or oval patties. (The mixture will be soft, so dampen your hands to help in the molding process.) Arrange the patties on an oven-proof plate that fits into a steamer (mine is bamboo).

4) Steam, covered, over boiling water for 6 to 7 minutes. They should still be moist in the center after steaming. Serve with the sauce.

Yield: 4 servings

COUSCOUS OF LOBSTER

This impressive dish combines lobster meat with flavorful couscous and is served with a fresh chive sauce. For a decorative presentation, the shells from the bodies of the lobsters can be used as receptacles. (Pictured on page 71.)

2　lobsters (2 lbs. each), preferably female

2　tablespoons virgin olive oil

1　medium onion, peeled and chopped (1 cup)

½　cup tomalley (liver) and coral (eggs), if lobster is a female

1½　cups (about 10 oz.) couscous

½　teaspoon salt

¼　teaspoon freshly ground black pepper

Chive Sauce

½　cup reduced lobster stock

¼　cup virgin olive oil

4　tablespoons finely minced chives

⅛　teaspoon salt

⅛　teaspoon freshly ground black pepper

COOKING LOBSTER
The lobster is cooked initially for only 8 minutes–just enough so that it can be removed from the shell. Then, just before serving, the lobster meat is reheated almost to a boil in the stock, and then set aside, for a few minutes, to finish cooking in the residual heat remaining in the hot poaching liquid. Avoid boiling the stock; it will toughen the lobster meat.

1) In a large stockpot, bring 3 quarts of water to a boil. Add the lobsters and bring water back to a boil. Boil gently for 8 minutes; remove and set aside. When cool enough to handle, remove the meat from the shells (reserving the shells from around the body) and set aside the tomalley and coral (about ½ cup combined).

2) To concentrate the taste of the stock, reduce it to 4 cups. You will need 1 cup to reheat the lobster meat and ½ cup for the sauce. Freeze the remainder.

For couscous:
1) Heat the 2 tablespoons of olive oil and sauté the onions over medium heat for about 2 minutes. Add the light green tomalley and dark green eggs and mix well, crushing the eggs with a fork. Stir in the couscous, and then add 1½ cups boiling water, ½ teaspoon salt and ¼ teaspoon pepper. Mix well. Remove from heat, cover; set aside for 10 minutes.

2) Combine the lobster meat with the 1 cup of reduced stock in a saucepan. Slowly bring stock almost to a boil and keep it at this temperature for 3 to 4 minutes, being careful that it does not boil.

For chive sauce:
1) Combine the stock, olive oil, chives, salt and pepper in a saucepan and bring to a strong boil.

2) Cut the reserved shells in half and fluff the couscous. Place some couscous on each plate and a shell receptacle on top. Fill the shell with couscous, arrange the warm lobster on top, and spoon sauce over to serve.

Yield: 4 servings

CATFISH ON RATATOUILLE

Farmed catfish are available now almost everywhere and, unlike their muddy-tasting pond relatives, these specimens are sweet-tasting. I coat the fish with an intensely flavored tarragon oil, made by combining tarragon leaves, chives, water, and a little olive oil together in a mini-chop or small food processor. The resulting green oil is not only beautiful but delicious with fish.

Ratatouille

4	tablespoons virgin olive oil
1	medium onion (4 oz.), peeled and chopped
1	small green bell pepper, cut into ½-inch pieces
1	zucchini (6 oz.), cut into ½-inch pieces
1	small eggplant (6 oz.), cut into ¾-inch pieces
1	large ripe tomato, halved, seeded and cut into ½-inch pieces
4	cloves garlic, peeled, crushed and finely chopped
¾	teaspoon salt
¼	teaspoon freshly ground black pepper

Tarragon Oil

2	tablespoons (loose) fresh tarragon leaves
2	tablespoons fresh chives, snipped
3	tablespoons water
2	tablespoons virgin olive oil
4	catfish fillets, cleaned of all yellow surface fat (about 7 oz. each)
¼	teaspoon salt

For ratatouille:
1) In a large skillet or saucepan, heat the olive oil and sauté the onion in the hot oil for 2 minutes. Add the eggplant and sauté for 2 minutes, then add the green pepper and zucchini and sauté for 1 minute longer. Stir in the tomatoes, garlic, salt, and pepper. Lower the heat, cover, and cook for 10 minutes. Set aside.

For tarragon oil:
1) Meanwhile, place the tarragon, chives, water, and olive oil in a mini-chop and process until liquified. Pour into a bowl. Set aside.

For catfish:
1) Place the catfish, salt, and ¼ cup water in a saucepan and bring to a boil. When boiling, reduce the heat, cover, and cook 3 minutes on the first side. Then turn and cook 3 minutes on the other side, or until tender.

2) To serve, divide the ratatouille between four plates and arrange a fish fillet on top of each portion. Coat lightly with the tarragon oil. Serve immediately.

Yield: 4 servings

CHICKEN & SEAFOOD PAELLA

Paella is a complete meal. It contains a lot of rice flavored with chorizo, the famed Spanish hot sausage; chicken legs; a seafood assortment of mussels, squid, and shrimp; and, finally, fresh vegetables. All of this is flavored, of course, with pistils from the crocus flower–what we call saffron–the best quality of which comes from Spain.This one-pot meal requires great attention to

3   ounces pancetta (best choice) or salt pork, cut into ¼-inch lardons (½ cup)

8   ounces chorizo (Spanish hot sausage), cut into 1-inch pieces

3   tablespoons virgin olive oil

3   chicken legs (about 1 lb.), skinned, carcass bone removed, and cut in half to separate thighs and drumsticks

1   medium onion (6 oz.), peeled and cut into ½-inch pieces (1¼ cups)

5   cloves garlic, peeled, crushed, and finely chopped (1½ tbs.)

2   cups long grain Carolina rice

½   cup (about ½ oz.) dry mushroom pieces

1   teaspoon (loose) saffron pistils, crushed between your thumb and fingers

1   teaspoon herbes de Provence

4   cups water

1   tomato (8 oz.), cut into ½-inch pieces (1⅓ cups)

1   red bell pepper (6 oz.), cut into ½-inch pieces

1) In a large saucepan, sauté the pork lardons and chorizos in olive oil for 5 minutes, partially covered to avoid splattering. Add the chicken and brown for 10 minutes over low to medium heat. Add the onions and garlic, and continue cooking for about 30 seconds.

2) Add the rice to the pot and mix it in well. Then stir in the mushrooms, saffron, herbes de Provence, water, tomato, red and Jalapeño peppers, salt, and pepper, and mix well. Bring to a boil, cover, reduce heat, and cook gently for 25 minutes.

3) Add the mussels, squid, and shrimp. Cook for 8 minutes. Then stir in the peas and asparagus and continue cooking, covered, for another 5 minutes.

4) Sprinkle with chives and serve with Tabasco sauce on the side.

Yield: 6 to 8 servings

· MAIN COURSE ·

timing. First, the pork and sausage are browned, and then, in their drippings, the chicken is browned. the rice is added next and cooked with the seasonings, and then the seafood is added. Finally, the asparagus and peas are placed in the pot. Staggering the ingredient additions in this way, everything is finished cooking at the same time. (Pictured on page 72.)

1	tablespoon chopped Jalapeño pepper
1	teaspoon salt
½	teaspoon freshly ground black pepper
1	pound (about 12) mussels
¾	pound squid (about 8 oz.), cleaned and cut into 1½-inch pieces
12	shrimp (about 8 oz.), shelled
½	cup fresh shelled or frozen baby peas
6	spears asparagus, cut into 1-inch pieces (1 cup)
1	tablespoon chopped chives
½	teaspoon Tabasco sauce

A SPANISH WORD
Paella comes from the Spanish word for the pan (usually a big iron or steel skillet or saucepan) in which this classic concoction is cooked. In keeping with tradition, people in Spain still often prepare this dish outdoors over a wood fire, bringing their chicken from the market and plucking it and cooking it with sausages and rice. Essentially, paella is a big stew of rice flavored with poultry, meat, seafood–whatever one can afford–with some vegetables added near the end of the cooking time.

CHICKEN LEGS WITH WINE & YAMS

This is one of those complete casserole dishes that makes a whole meal by itself. I use chicken legs for this dish because they stew better than chicken breasts, which tend to get stringy. Notice, however, that I remove the skin from the legs, which eliminates most of the fat.One chicken leg per person is sufficient when the legs are divided into thighs and drumsticks, especially since there are several vegetable garnishes as well.

4	chicken legs (about 3 lbs. total)
2	tablespoons virgin olive oil
¼	cup chopped onion
4	large shallots (about 6 oz.), peeled
8	medium mushrooms (about 5 oz.)
4	yams (about 1 lb.), peeled and halved lengthwise
1	cup dry white wine
8	large garlic cloves, peeled
½	teaspoon salt
½	teaspoon freshly ground black pepper
2	tablespoons chopped parsley, for garnish

1) Remove the skin from the chicken legs, using a kitchen towel to help pull it off. In some markets, chicken legs are packaged with a piece of back carcass attached to the joint of the pelvis. If this is the case, remove any attached carcass bones from the chicken legs and then separate the legs into thighs and drumsticks.

2) Heat the olive oil in one large or two smaller skillets and brown the chicken pieces (partially covered to prevent splattering) on all sides for about 10 minutes.

3) Add the onion and cook for 1 minute, then add the shallots, mushrooms, yams, wine, garlic, salt and pepper.

4) Bring to a boil, cover, and boil very gently for 20 minutes. Garnish with parsley and serve.

Yield: 4 servings

CHICKEN IN TARRAGON SAUCE

This is an elegant dish that you can make easily and quickly if you buy skinless chicken breasts from the supermarket. I add some cream at the end here, and garnish the dish with fresh tarragon, which goes particularly well with the chicken and cream.

6	pieces of skinless chicken (2 drumsticks and 2 thighs with bones left in, and 2 boneless breasts)
½	cup dry, fruity white wine
1	small onion (about 3 oz.), chopped (¾ cup)
½	cup good quality chicken stock, preferably homemade (see Chicken Broth, page 30)
2	bay leaves
1	sprig fresh thyme
½	teaspoon salt
¼	teaspoon freshly ground black pepper
1	teaspoon potato starch dissolved in 1 tablespoon water
¼	cup heavy cream
1	teaspoon chopped fresh tarragon, for garnish

1) Place the chicken drumsticks, thighs, wine, onion, stock, bay leaves, thyme, salt, and pepper in a saucepan, and bring to a boil. Reduce the heat, cover and boil gently for about 10 minutes.

2) Add the breast meat, cover and boil gently for another 10 minutes.

3) Transfer the meat to a dish and keep warm. Measure the cooking liquid. There should be about 1 cup; if there is more, reduce it to 1 cup.

4) Stir in the dissolved potato starch, bring to a boil, and then add the cream and return to the boil. Return the chicken pieces to the pan and heat them through. Remove from the heat, sprinkle with the tarragon and serve.

Yield: 4 servings

TIMING TIP
Notice that the dark meat is cooked for about 20 minutes and the breast meat is cooked for only 10 minutes. Delaying the addition of the white meat prevents it from becoming overcooked, which makes it stringy.

GRILLED CHICKEN WITH CABBAGE ANCHOYADE

In this recipe, the chicken breasts are marinated for several hours in a finely chopped mixture of oregano, lemon skin, black pepper, and olive oil. A mini-chop, smaller and faster than a food processor, is ideal to chop the herbs. Cooked on a hot grill, the breasts will brown quickly and remain moist in the center. (Pictured on page 1.)

8	strips lemon peel, removed with a vegetable peeler
2	teaspoons black peppercorns
4	tablespoons (loose) fresh oregano
4	boneless skinless chicken breasts (about 8 oz. each), from roasting chickens
3	tablespoons virgin olive oil
1	teaspoon salt

Cabbage Anchoyade

4	cloves garlic, peeled, crushed and finely chopped (about 2 tsp.)
6	anchovy fillets, chopped fine (4 tsp.)
½	teaspoon salt
½	teaspoon freshly ground black pepper
½	red bell pepper, peeled and cut into ¼-inch dice (½ cup)
4	teaspoons red wine vinegar
4	tablespoons virgin olive oil
18	ounces Savoy cabbage, shredded (8 cups)

1) Place the lemon strips, peppercorns and oregano in the bowl of a mini-chop, and process to a powder (about 4 tbs). Sprinkle the mixture over the chicken and arrange it in a dish. Sprinkle with the olive oil. Cover, and set aside in the refrigerator to macerate for at least ½ hour or as long as overnight.

2) At cooking time, sprinkle the chicken with salt and arrange it on a hot grill. Cook about 4 minutes on each side, and transfer to a warm oven (180°) until serving time (up to 1 hour ahead).

For cabbage anchoyade:
1) In a bowl, combine garlic, anchovies, salt, pepper, red bell pepper (reserving 1 tablespoon for garnish), vinegar and oil. Add the cabbage, and mix well. (This can be made up to 3 to 4 hours ahead and refrigerated until serving time.)

2) At serving time, arrange the cabbage mixture in a mound in the center of four serving plates. Slice the chicken breasts lengthwise and arrange the meat all around and on top of the cabbage. Sprinkle with reserved red bell pepper and serve immediately.

Yield: 4 servings

· MAIN COURSE ·

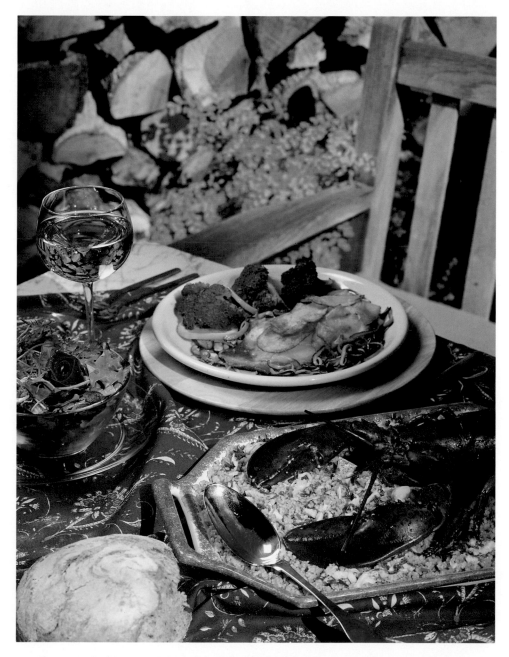

From top: Red Snapper in Potato Jacket with Broccoli Piquante and Couscous of Lobster.

· MAIN COURSE ·

Clockwise from top: Chicken & Seafood Paella; Grilled Quail on Quinoa with Sunflower Seeds and Poulet au Vin Rouge.

· MAIN COURSE ·

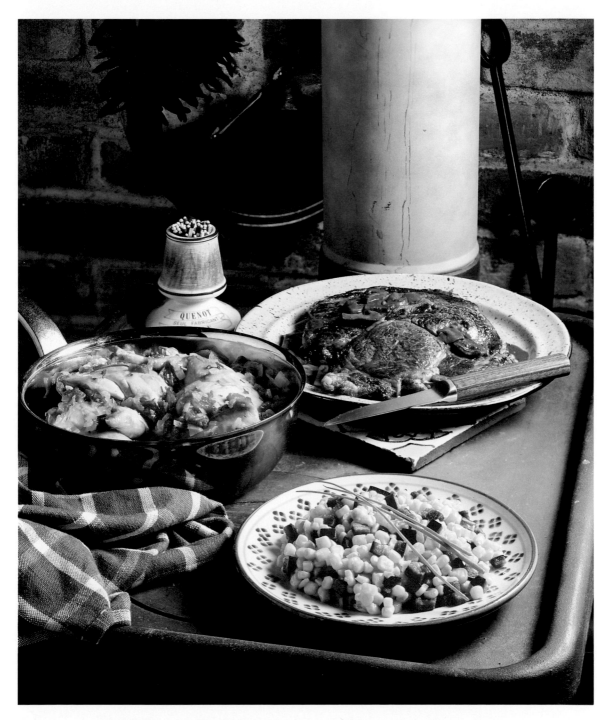

Clockwise from top: Wine Merchant Steak; Corn & Pepper Sauté and Ragout of Rabbit.

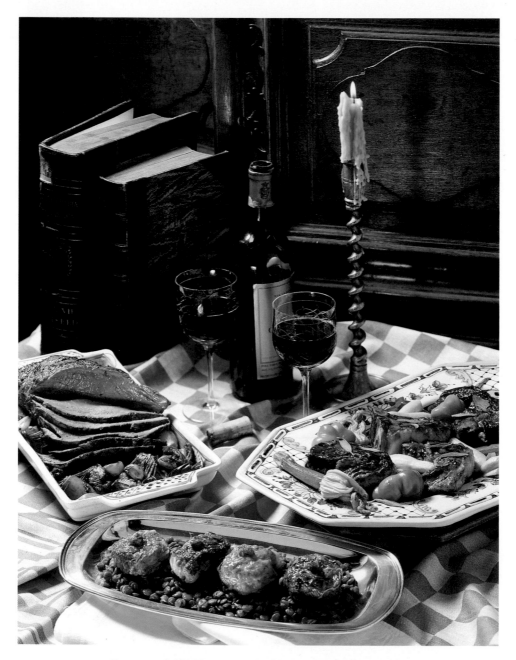

From top: Grilled Savory Lamb Chops with Baby Vegetables;
Saucisses au Chou on Lentils and Veal Roast with Artichokes.

POULE AU POT

*P**oule* is actually the French name for "hen," and this famous "chicken in a pot" dish originated in the 16th century under the rule of Henry IV. Conventionally, it is not as refined as I make it here by removing the meat from the bones and making the stock fat free. Notice that everything is used, including the stock in which the chicken is cooked, so there is no loss of nutrients or vitamins.

1   **chicken (about 3½ lbs.)**
1   **teaspoon dried thyme leaves**
1   **teaspoon dried rosemary**
3   **bay leaves**
12 **cloves**
2   **teaspoon salt**
1   **teaspoon black peppercorns**

Vegetables
2   **large leeks (about 12 oz.), cleaned**
4   **medium onions (10 oz. total), peeled**
4   **carrots (about 1 lb.), peeled**
1   **small butternut squash (1 lb.), peeled, seeded, and quartered**
1   **small Savoy cabbage (about 1 lbs.), quartered**
4   **large mushrooms (about 4 oz.)**

16 **slices (2 oz.) from a baguette, toasted in the oven**
½   **cup grated Gruyère cheese**
    Cornichons and hot mustard

A WORD ABOUT STOCK
The stock is strained through paper towels to eliminate as much fat as possible, but if time permits, it's a good idea to chill it and remove and discard additional fat that solidifies on top.

1) Place the chicken, breast side down, with the neck and heart in a narrow stainless steel stock pot. (Reserve the liver to sauté or freeze for future use.) Add 4 quarts of water, and bring it to a boil over high heat. Reduce heat and boil gently for 10 minutes. Skim the cooking liquid to remove fat and impurities that come to the surface.

2) Add the thyme, rosemary, bay leaves, cloves, salt, and peppercorns to the stock . Cover and continue boiling gently for 25 minutes (for a total of 35 minutes). Remove the chicken from the pot. When it is cool enough to handle, pull off and discard the skin. Pull meat from bones, keeping it in the largest possible pieces. Set meat aside, covered, in about ½ cup of the stock. Place bones back in the remaining stock and boil gently for another hour.

3) Strain stock twice through a strainer lined with paper towels. Rinse out the pot and return the stock to the pot. You should have 8 to 9 cups. (If necessary, adjust with water.)

For vegetables:
1) Add leeks, onions, carrots, squash and cabbage to stock, and bring to the boil. Boil, covered, for 15 minutes. Add mushrooms and cook for another 5 minutes.

2) Reheat the meat and surrounding liquid and arrange it in the center of a large platter. Remove the vegetables with a slotted spoon and arrange them around the chicken. Ladle some of the stock into small bowls and serve it with the croutons and cheese; pass around cornichons and hot mustard at the table.

Yield: 4 to 6 servings

POULET AU VIN ROUGE

This is a modern version of the classic *coq au vin*–rich in flavor but lower in calories than the original, and much faster to make. I divide the chicken into pieces, remove the skin, brown it, and cook it in red wine, adding the breast pieces at the end so they don't overcook. The onions are

1	chicken (3½ to 4 lbs.)
12	small pearl onions (6 oz.), peeled
2	tablespoons virgin olive oil
½	cup water
½	teaspoon sugar
4	large mushrooms (4 oz.), quartered
⅓	cup finely chopped onion
3	cloves garlic, peeled, crushed and finely chopped (2 tsp.)
1¼	cups dry, fruity red wine
½	teaspoon dried thyme leaves or 1 sprig fresh thyme
2	bay leaves
¾	teaspoon salt
¾	teaspoon freshly ground black pepper
1	teaspoon potato starch dissolved in 2 tablespoons red wine

1) Cut the chicken into 4 pieces (2 breasts with wings, and 2 legs). Cut off the wings and divide them at the joints into 3 pieces. Skin and bone the breasts. Set the breasts aside with the two meatier wing pieces. (Freeze the bones and wing tips for future use.) Skin the legs and separate the thighs from the drumsticks by cutting through them at the joint. Cut the ends off the drumsticks. The thigh and drum bones should be left in. Set the legs aside with the breasts and reserved wing pieces.

2) Place the pearl onions with 1 tablespoon of the olive oil, the sugar, and ½ cup water in a large saucepan, and bring to a boil over high heat. Boil for a few minutes, or until the water has evaporated and the onions start frying. Cook until the onions are browned on all sides. Add the mushrooms and sauté for 1 minute. Set aside, covered.

3) In a large skillet, heat the remaining 1 table-spoon olive oil. When hot, sauté the chicken wing pieces for 2 to 3 minutes, until lightly browned on all sides. Add the legs pieces and brown them for about 2 to 3 minutes on each side. Repeat with the breasts. Set all the chicken pieces aside.

4) To the drippings in the skillet, add the chopped onions and sauté them for 1 minute, then add the garlic and cook for about 10 seconds. Add the wine, thyme, bay leaves, salt, and pepper, and bring to a boil. Return the dark meat and the wings to the pan, cover, and boil very gently for 8 minutes.

glazed separately in a little olive oil and sugar, with the mushrooms added near the end of the cooking time. Finally, everything is combined together and served with croutons. (Pictured on page 72.)

Croutons
1	teaspoon canola oil
4	slices white bread
2	tablespoons chopped parsley

5) Then add the chicken breasts, and boil gently for another 7 minutes. This brings the total cooking time to 15 minutes for the dark meat, and only 7 minutes for the breast meat.

6) Add the dissolved potato starch to the pan and stir until the pan juices are thickened, then add the pearl onions and mushrooms with their juices to the red wine sauce.

For croutons:
1) Trim the crusts from the bread, and cut the slices diagonally into triangles. Trim each triangle to form a heart-shaped crouton.

2) Spread the teaspoon of oil on a cookie sheet and press the croutons into the oil so they are moistened on both sides. Place in a 400° oven for 8 to 10 minutes, until nicely browned.

3) To serve, cut the chicken breast pieces in half and serve one piece of breast, one piece of drum or thigh meat, and one piece of wing per person with two croutons, first dipping the tip of each crouton in the sauce to moisten it, and then into the chopped parsley. Sprinkle the remaining chopped parsley over the chicken and garnishes.

Yield: 4 servings

A MODERN VERSION
Poulet au Vin Rouge is a classic *coq au vin*, although historically the "cock"–an older chicken–was so tough that it had to be cooked a long time and then the juices were thickened with the blood of the chicken. Now, with the tender chickens we have available, this dish can be made quickly The skin of the chicken is removed and the meat cooked in red wine. Happily, more than 50 per cent of the wine's calories disappear through the cooking process.

BROWN RICE CHICKEN FRICASSEE

For this fricassee, I use short grain brown rice, which takes about an hour to cook. To reduce the cooking time by 15 minutes, substitute medium grain white rice. Only the wing pieces have skin on them, but these render enough fat to brown the rest of the bones. Use a sturdy skillet to cook the bones long enough so that they are nicely browned.

About 1¾ pounds chicken bones, including neck, gizzard, and wing sections

1   large onion (6 oz.), peeled and coarsely chopped (1¼ cups)

1½ cups short grain brown rice

1   ripe tomato, chopped or 1 cup drained canned tomato, crushed

2   to 3 cloves garlic, peeled, crushed and finely chopped

1   small Jalapeño pepper, seeded and chopped (2 tsp.)

¼   cup coarsely chopped cilantro with stems

1   teaspoon salt

¼   teaspoon freshly ground black pepper

¾   cup Spanish salad olives, cut into ½-inch pieces

⅓   cup dark raisins

3   cups water

1) In a large saucepan, sauté the chicken bones over medium to high heat for 15 minutes until nicely browned.

2) Add the onions and sauté 1 minute, then stir in the rice.

3) Add the tomatoes, garlic, Jalapeño pepper, cilantro, salt, pepper, olives, raisins, and water, and bring the mixture to a boil. Reduce the heat, cover, and boil gently for 50 minutes.

4) Remove the bones, and when cold enough to handle, pick the meat from them and return it to the dish. Serve.

Yield: 6 servings

CLAUDINE'S FRICASSEE
My daughter, Claudine, has a favorite chicken fricassee dish, too. In her version, cooked chicken gizzards are combined with the same rice, garlic and onion that I use but she flavors her fricassee with cilantro and extends it with zucchini and eggplant.

· MAIN COURSE ·

GRILLED QUAIL ON QUINOA WITH SUNFLOWER SEEDS

*Q*uinoa, a grain that dates back to the Incas, is one of the super grains of the future, high not only in fiber but in Vitamins A and B and phosphorous. As quinoa cooks, it becomes almost transparent. I have added sautéed sunflower seed and dried currants in this recipe that features grilled boneless quail. (Pictured on page 72.)

Marinade

1	medium-size shallot, peeled
1	large clove garlic, peeled
1	tablespoon fish sauce (nuocmam)
½	teaspoon sugar
¼	of a small Jalapeño pepper
1	tablespoon water
4	boneless quail (about 4 oz. each)

Quinoa

2	tablespoons peanut oil
1	small onion, chopped (about ½ cup)
2	tablespoons sunflower (or pumpkin) seeds, hulled
2	tablespoons dried currants
1	cup (6 oz.) quinoa
1¾	cups chicken stock, preferably homemade (see Chicken Broth, page 30)
¾	teaspoon salt
¼	teaspoon freshly ground black pepper

1) Place the shallots, garlic, fish sauce, sugar, Jalapêno pepper, and water in a small mini-chop, and process until liquified. Place the quail in a flat dish and pour overt marinade, turning until coated. Cover and refrigerate for at least one hour.

2) At cooking time, place the quail on a very hot grill and cook 2½ to 3 minutes on each side. Transfer to a dish and keep warm in a 180° oven until serving time (up to 45 minutes).

For quinoa:

1) Heat the oil in a skillet and when hot, sauté the onions and seeds for 2 minutes.

2) Add the currants and quinoa and mix well. Stir in the stock, salt and pepper. Bring to a boil, reduce the heat, cover, and boil gently for about 18 minutes, until fluffy and tender.

For grilling quail:

1) Place quail on very hot grill and cook 2 to 3 minutes on each side. Transfer to a dish and keep warm in a 180° oven.

2) Arrange quinoa in the center of individual plates and place a quail on top. Pour any natural juices over the the quail that have accumulated in the dish.

Yield: 4 servings

ROASTED TURKEY WITH MUSHROOM STUFFING

On holidays, I like to serve a small roasted turkey with whole wheat stuffing flavored with golden raisins and dried mushrooms, which have a highly concentrated taste. Be sure to use the soaking liquid from the mushrooms to moisten the stuffing. Begin by roasting the turkey, breast-side-up

1	11-pound turkey
½	teaspoon salt
½	teaspoon freshly ground black pepper
3	onions (about 12 oz.), peeled and cut into 1-inch dice
10	cloves garlic, unpeeled
1	teaspoon potato starch dissolved in 1 tablespoon water
1	tablespoon soy sauce

For turkey:

1) Reserve the turkey liver for another use and place the neck, gizzard, and heart in a saucepan with 2 cups of water. Bring to a boil, cover, reduce the heat, and cook over low heat for about 1 hour. Drain, reserving the cooking liquids and the solids separately. You should have about 1½ cups of cooking liquid. Set aside. Pull the meat from the neck bones and cut it with the gizzard and heart into a ¼-inch dice. Place in a bowl and reserve.

2) Preheat oven to 425°. Sprinkle the turkey inside and out with the salt and pepper and place it breast-side-up in a large roasting pan. Bake for 30 minutes.

3) Then, using pot holders, turn the turkey so it is breast-side-down. Arrange the onions and garlic cloves around it. Reduce the oven temperature to 350°. Return turkey to the oven and cook for 1½ hours, then add the 1½ cups reserved cooking liquid (from the neck, gizzard, and heart), turn the turkey so it is breast-side-up, and continue cooking it for ½ hour longer to brown the breast. Turn the oven off, transfer the turkey to an ovenproof platter, and return it to the warm oven to rest.

For stuffing:

1) Place the mushrooms in a bowl and add the water. Set aside for at least 30 minutes. Drain, press (reserving the soaking liquid in the bowl), and coarsely chop the mushrooms, and set them aside with the soaking liquid.

2) Heat the oils in a large skillet or saucepan. When hot, sauté the onions and celery for 3 minutes. Add

at a high temperature about 30 minutes, or until the skin is brown and crispy. Turn the turkey over, reduce the heat, and continue roasting it upside-down (so that the juices flow through the breasts). Near the end of cooking time, invert the turkey again, to re-brown the breast skin.

Stuffing

¾   cup dried mushroom pieces, preferably cepes (about ¾ oz.)

1½ cups warm water, for soaking mushrooms

2   tablespoons virgin olive oil

2   tablespoons canola oil

1   medium onion (6 oz.), peeled and chopped fine (1¼ cups)

1   to 2 stalks celery (white, from inside), chopped (½ cup)

½   teaspoon herbes de Provence

3   cloves garlic, peeled, crushed and finely chopped (2 tsp.)

6   slices (about 7 oz.) sprouted wheat bread (wholewheat bread made with wheat kernels)

⅓   cup golden raisins

½   teaspoon salt

¼   teaspoon freshly ground black pepper

the herbes de Provence, garlic, and mushrooms, mix well, and remove from the heat. Toast the bread slices well, and cut them into ⅜-inch croutons. (You should have 3 cups.) Stir the croutons and raisins into the mixture in the skillet.

3) Pour the reserved mushroom soaking liquid into a measuring cup, leaving behind and discarding the sandy residue in the bottom of the bowl. (You should have about ¾ cup.)

4) Add to the mixture in the skillet with the salt and pepper, and toss gently to combine. Pack lightly into a loaf pan and cover with aluminum foil. Bake in a preheated 400° oven for 30 minutes.

For gravy:

1) Push the vegetables and cooking juices from the roasting pan through a sieve or a food mill (if you want to include the puréed vegetables in your gravy) into a saucepan.

2) Let rest for 4 to 5 minutes, until most of the fat has risen to the top, and skim off as much of it as possible. You should have approximately 2 cups of cooking juices.

3) Add the reserved diced neck, gizzard, and heart meat, and simmer the mixture for 10 minutes to reduce it slightly. Stir in the dissolved potato starch and soy sauce until smooth.

4) Carve the turkey and serve it with the gravy and mushroom stuffing.

Yield: 8 to 10 servings

RAGOUT OF RABBIT

This recipe exemplifies the earthy country cooking of France. After dry roasting the rabbit in a large skillet for about 30 minutes, until it is almost cooked, I make an appealing sauce with the solidified pan juices, garlic, onions, tomatoes, and a reduction of vinegar. (Pictured on page 73.)

1	tablespoon unsalted butter
2	tablespoons virgin olive oil
1	young rabbit (about 2½ lbs.), cut into 10 to 12 pieces
¾	teaspoon salt
¾	teaspoon freshly ground black pepper
5	to 6 cloves garlic, peeled, crushed and chopped (2 tbs.)
2	onions (6 oz.), peeled and chopped (1⅓ cups)
¼	cup red wine vinegar
1	ripe tomato, coarsely chopped (1 cup)
1	tablespoon chopped chives, for garnish

1) Heat the butter and the oil in a 12-inch skillet. Season the rabbit pieces with ½ teaspoon each of the salt and pepper.

2) Arrange rabbit pieces in the skillet and brown them, covered, over medium to high heat for 40 minutes, turning them every 10 minutes. (Add a few tablespoons of water if the pan becomes so dry that the rabbit starts burning.) The rabbit exterior should be crusty and brown and the juices well crystallized.

3) Transfer the rabbit to a dish, and add the garlic and onions to the juices in the pan. Sauté for 2 to 3 minutes, then add the vinegar and cook, stirring to dissolve the solidified juices, for about 2 minutes or until the mixture is reduced to a glaze.

4) Add the tomatoes and remaining salt and pepper. Return the rabbit to the sauce and heat gently for 2 to 3 minutes. Sprinkle with chives and serve immediately.

Yield: 4 servings

A WORD ABOUT RABBIT
Although rabbit, high in protein and low in fat, is still considered an esoteric meat in some parts of the U.S., it is a commonly eaten throughout Europe, where young rabbits are either roasted whole or sautéed dry, as mine is here. Older, tougher specimens are used in stew or braised.
If you cannot find a rabbit of approximately the same size as I use here, select one (or two, if they are very small) that is less than three months old.

VEAL CHOPS WITH MUSHROOMS

I use relatively small veal chops here, each weighing about ½ pound with the bone. Veal is low in calories and most markets offer a good quality, milk-fed variety. If you can, buy it occasionally, as I do, from farms that feed their cows organic foods. The quality is dramatically better. The mushrooms are sautéed in the veal drippings, creating a delicious sauce for serving on the chops.

2	teaspoons virgin olive oil
2	teaspoons unsalted butter
4	veal loin chops, about ¾-inch thick (8 oz. each), preferably white milk-fed veal, called plume de veau, Provimi, or Nature Veal
½	teaspoon salt
½	teaspoon freshly ground black pepper
2	shallots, peeled and chopped (¼ cup)
12	ounces mushrooms, sliced (about 5 cups)
¼	cup dry white wine
2	cloves garlic, peeled, crushed and finely chopped (1 tsp.)
¼	cup chopped parsley

1) Heat the oil and butter in a large skillet. Sprinkle the veal chops with half the salt and pepper, and sauté in the hot oil and butter for 4 minutes on each side. Remove to a platter.

2) In the pan drippings, sauté the shallots for 10 seconds over medium heat. Add the mushrooms and wine, and cook, covered, for 1 minute.

3) Then uncover and cook for another minute. Add the garlic and remaining salt and pepper. Toss and cook for 10 seconds, then stir in the parsley. Pour the mushroom sauce over the veal chops. Serve immediately.

Yield: 4 servings

ROAST OF VEAL WITH ARTICHOKES

A piece of shoulder is the best choice for this recipe. Sometimes, if you buy the large muscle of the shoulder, you don't have to tie the meat; if, however, the piece is separating or is longer and flatter, it should be rolled and tied with twine. If you are in a part of the U.S. where you can obtain baby artichokes, use them instead of the large ones, cutting them into halves rather than quarters. Also, if you don't find the larger pearl onions I used here, substitute more of the smaller ones. This roast is good served cold with a green salad, tomato salad, or pasta salad.

2½ **pound boneless veal shoulder roast, trimmed of most surface fat (Note: My roast was about 8½ inches long by 2½ inches in diameter.)**

½ **teaspoon salt**

½ **teaspoon freshly ground black pepper**

1 **teaspoon dried thyme leaves**

1 **tablespoon unsalted butter**

1 **tablespoon virgin olive oil**

5 **medium artichokes, with stems (about 1 lb. 12 oz.)**

12 **onions (14 oz.), each about the size of a ping-pong ball, peeled**

18 **large cloves garlic, peeled**

1 **tomato (6 oz.), cut in half, seeded, and cut into ½ inch pieces (1 cup)**

1 **tablespoon soy sauce**

2 **tablespoons water**

1) Tie the trimmed roast with twine if necessary, and sprinkle it with ¼ teaspoon each of the salt and pepper, and the thyme. In an ovenproof skillet heat the butter and oil. When hot, add the meat, and brown it on all sides for a total of 8 to 10 minutes. Remove the roast to a platter and reserve the drippings in the skillet.

2) With a sharp knife, remove the top third of the artichokes. Then, trim off the upper half of remaining leaves with scissors to remove the thorny projections. Cut the artichokes into fourths, and remove and discard the chokes.

3) Add the artichokes, onions, garlic, and remaining salt and pepper to the drippings it the skillet, and toss the vegetables to coat them with the drippings. Arrange the roast on top of the vegetables and place the pan in a 400° oven for 20 minutes. Turn the roast over, stirring the vegetables as you do so, and return the pan to the oven for another 20 minutes. Stir in the tomatoes, soy sauce, and water, and cook for 10 additional minutes, for a total cooking time of 1 hour (not including the browning).*

4) Remove the roast from the oven and allow it to rest for 10 minutes before carving and serving.

Yield: 4 servings

*Note: If your roast is shorter and thicker than mine (see ingredient listing), cook it a little longer.

· MAIN COURSE ·

WINE MERCHANT STEAK

The steaks in this classic bistro dish are relatively small compared to those served a few years ago. In addition, they are trimmed of all fat, leaving them with a weight of about 7 ounces each, an ample serving. Although the steaks can be grilled and served plain, I extend the dish with a sauce made of shallots, mushrooms, garlic, and a good, earthy wine, thickened with Dijon mustard, and garnished with chopped chives. (Pictured on page 73.)

4   New York strip, shell, or sirloin tip steaks (9 oz. each), about ¾-inch thick

¾   teaspoon salt

½   teaspoon freshly ground black pepper

2   tablespoons virgin olive oil

2   shallots, peeled and chopped fine (4 tbs.)

4   large mushrooms (about 4 oz.),julienned

2   large cloves garlic, peeled, crushed and chopped fine (1½ tsp.)

1   cup red wine (beaujolais-type)

1   cup chicken broth, preferably homemade (see Chicken Broth, page 30)

1   tablespoon Worcestershire sauce

1   tablespoon Dijon-style mustard

½   teaspoon potato starch dissolved in 2 teaspoons water

1   tablespoon finely chopped chives

1) Trim the steaks, removing all visible surface fat and sinews. The trimmed steaks should weigh about 7 ounces each.

2) Sprinkle the steaks with ½ teaspoon of the salt and the pepper.

3) Heat the olive oil in a large skillet; when hot, add the steaks and sauté for 2½ minutes on each side for medium rare.

4) Remove the steaks to a platter and set aside in a warm place. To the drippings in the skillet, add the shallots and sauté for about 10 seconds. Add the mushrooms and garlic, and sauté for 1 minute. Stir in the wine, and boil it down until only about 2 tablespoons remain. Add the stock, and reduce the mixture to about ¾ cup.

5) Add the Worcestershire sauce, mustard, and remaining salt, and mix well. Stir in the dissolved potato starch and bring the mixture to a boil.

6) Arrange the steaks on individual plates and spoon some sauce on top and around each steak. Garnish with the chives and serve.

Yield: 4 servings

SPICY BEEF SHELL ROAST

If you allow only a small portion of meat per serving, and trim it completely, beef is a perfectly acceptable component of well balanced diet. It is, in fact, a good source of iron. Moreover, using dry herbs, as I do here to flavor the meat, enables me to cut back on the amount of salt I use. Notice that the beef is cooked initially on top of the stove before it is finished in the oven; this produces an exterior crust that intensifies the taste of the meat.

1	beef shell roast (also called New York strip), about 1½ pounds untrimmed
1	teaspoon dried thyme
1	teaspoon dried oregano
1	teaspoon dried rosemary
¼	teaspoon freshly ground black pepper
¼	teaspoon cayenne pepper
¼	teaspoon salt
1	tablespoon virgin olive oil
¼	cup chicken stock

1) Remove all surface fat from the roast. The trimmed roast should weigh 1¼ pounds and be 1¾-inches thick.

2) Crush the dried herbs between your thumb and finger, and mix them with the black and cayenne peppers. Pat the mixture on both sides of the meat.

3) When ready to cook, sprinkle the roast with the salt. Heat the oil in a heavy ovenproof skillet or saucepan. When hot, add the meat and cook over medium to high heat for 3 minutes on each side.

4) Then transfer roast to a preheated 450° oven and cook for 8 to 10 minutes for medium rare. Add the chicken stock and let rest 10 minutes before carving. Serve with the natural meat cooking juices.

Yield: 4 servings

GRILLED SAVORY LAMB CHOPS

These are best cooked on a very hot grill, so start your fire early enough so that it is generating a lot of heat when you are ready to cook. Without the bone, these chops would each weigh only about 4 ounces, which is adequate when they are served with vegetables or other dishes. (Pictured on page 74.)

4   lamb chops, about 1½-inches thick (6 oz. each), well trimmed

¼   teaspoon freshly ground black pepper

2   tablespoons chopped fresh savory

1   tablespoon virgin olive oil

½   teaspoon salt

1) Sprinkle the chops on both sides with the pepper and the savory.

2) Pour the olive oil onto a plate and dip the chops, one side and then the other, in the oil.

3) Arrange the chops on the plate, cover with plastic wrap, and refrigerate until ready to cook later that day.

4) At cooking time, sprinkle the chops with salt. Cook over high heat on a grill for about 3½ to 4 minutes on each side for medium rare meat.

5) Transfer to a warm oven and allow the chops to "rest" for a few minutes before serving.

Yield: 4 servings

A WORD ABOUT LAMB CHOPS
Loin chops are readily available at supermarkets. They have a small T-bone in them and are more meaty than rib lamb chops. Trim off any large pieces of outside fat, sprinkle with the seasonings and oil, and either cook them immediately or allow them to macerate, refrigerated, until cooking time.

IRISH LAMB STEW

In this recipe, the vegetable garnishes are cooked separately in water, and then that water, which contains all the vegetables' nutrients, is used to cook the lamb. The trimmings from these vegetables are added to the stew and become the thickening agent for a gravy made from the natural cooking juices. This makes for a flavorful and hearty dish that is also low in calories and fat.

1½ pounds potatoes

3 carrots (about 10 oz.)

3 to 4 ribs celery (about 5 oz.)

1½ pounds lamb from the leg or shoulder, well trimmed and cut into 1-inch cubes

2 medium onions (about 8 oz.), peeled and quartered

3 large cloves garlic, peeled

3 sprigs fresh thyme or 1 teaspoon dried thyme

2 bay leaves

1 teaspoon salt

½ teaspoon freshly ground black pepper

2 teaspoons Worcestershire sauce

1 tablespoon chopped parsley

1) Peel the potatoes and cut them into 18 pieces of about equal size. Round off the cut corners of each potato piece and reserve the trimmings. You should have about 2 cups of trimmings and 18 small, "roundish" potatoes, all approximately the same size. Peel the carrots and cut them into sticks 1¾-inches long by ½-inch thick. Trim the celery ribs (reserving the trimmings) and cut them into sticks 2 inches long by ½-inch wide.

2) Place the potatoes in a saucepan and add 3 cups of water. Bring to a boil, reduce the heat, and boil gently, covered, for 12 minutes. Drain, reserving the cooking liquid, and set the potatoes aside. Return the reserved cooking liquid to the saucepan, add the carrots and celery, and bring back to the boil. Boil gently for 5 minutes. Drain, reserving the cooking liquid. (You should have about 2 cups of liquid; adjust with water as needed.)

3) Place the lamb in a Dutch oven or cooking pot with a tight-fitting lid and add the reserved cooking liquid and the potato and celery trimmings. Then, stir in the onions, garlic, thyme, bay leaves, salt, pepper, and Worcestershire, and bring to a boil. Reduce heat, cover and boil gently for 45 minutes.

4) Remove the meat, push the cooking juices and vegetable pieces through a food mill (or process momentarily in a food processor), and place them back in the pot with the meat. Add the reserved small potatoes, the celery, and the carrot sticks to the pot, and bring to a boil. Simmer 5 minutes. Sprinkle with parsley, and serve immediately,

Yield: 6 servings

GRILLED LEG OF LAMB

In this recipe, a mini-chop comes in handy to reduce the marinade ingredients to a purée. The lamb can be marinated for up to a day, at least for a few hours before it is grilled. If you don't have a grill, you can cook the meat under your oven broiler. After grilling, the lamb is transferred to a warm oven, where it finishes cooking in its own residual heat.

Marinade

24 mint leaves (about ⅓ cup, lightly packed)

½ small Jalapeño pepper (about the value of 2 tsp.)

1 piece ginger (about the value of 1 tbs.), peeled

2 cloves garlic, peeled

2 tablespoons apricot jam

1 tablespoon soy sauce

3 tablespoons water

1½ pound piece boneless lamb from the back leg, trimmed of most of the fat

1) Place the mint leaves, Jalapeño pepper, ginger, garlic, jam, soy sauce, and water in the bowl of mini-chop, and process until liquified.

2) Transfer to a plastic bag. Place the lamb in the bag with the seasonings and seal the bag. Refrigerate for at least 2 hours or overnight to allow the meat to macerate in the seasonings.

3) To cook, remove the lamb from the bag and dry it off with paper towels.

4) Place it on a grill over very high heat for about 7 minutes on each side. Then, transfer the meat to a roasting pan, pour the reserved marinade around it, and place it in a 200° oven for at least 15 minutes.

5) Slice and serve with some of the juices.

Yield: 4 servings

SAUCISSES AU CHOU ON LENTILS

It is best to buy a lean piece of pork and grind it yourself for the sausage patties in this recipe. Highly seasoned with coriander, cumin, and hot pepper, the patties are wrapped in blanched Savoy cabbage leaves, so the meat stays juicy and moist as it cooks. If you don't have access to a grill, sauté six patties at a time in a non-stick pan, cooking them in 2 teaspoons of safflower oil for about 5 minutes on each side.

Sausage Mixture

1¼ pounds lean ground pork

1½ teaspoons salt

¼ teaspoon freshly ground black pepper

¾ teaspoon fennel seed

½ teaspoon ground coriander seeds

½ teaspoon ground cumin

⅛ teaspoon cayenne pepper

⅛ teaspoon ground allspice

½ cup coarsely chopped mushrooms (about 2 oz.)

6 large outer leaves from a Savoy cabbage (about 10 oz.)

For sausage patties:

1) Thoroughly mix the sausage ingredients together in a bowl and refrigerate, covered. (This should be done a minimum of 2 hours before cooking so the seasonings can flavor the meat well. If prepared one day ahead, reserve the mushrooms, which might darken and discolor the mixture, and mix them in just before forming the mixture into patties.)

2) In a large saucepan, bring 6 cups of water to a boil, add the cabbage leaves, and bring the water back to the boil.

3) Cook the cabbage for 5 minutes, until soft but still firm. Drain and refresh under cool water.

4) Cut each leaf on either side of the center stem. Discard the stems (or add them to soup). Form the sausage mixture into patties about 1½ to 2 ounces each, and wrap each patty in a piece of cooked cabbage leaf. You should have 12 patties.

For lentils:

1) Wash the lentils under cool, running water and place them in a pot with the water, onions, 2 teaspoons of the chopped garlic, bay leaves, and salt.

2) Bring to a boil, cover, and boil gently for 20 to 25 minutes. The lentils should be tender and a little wet; if there is an excess of liquid remaining, drain it off. (One cup of raw lentils will yield 3 cups of cooked lentils.)

· MAIN COURSE ·

In this recipe, lentils, very high in soluble fibers, are cooked with seasonings and then combined with a little olive oil, garlic, pepper, Tabasco, and mustard. These could be served on their own as a first course or as an meat accompaniment. (Pictured on page 74.)

Lentils

½ pound (1 cup) lentils

3 cups water

2 small onions (4 oz.), peeled and chopped (¾ cup)

4 large cloves garlic, peeled, crushed and finely chopped (3 tsp.)

2 bay leaves

¾ teaspoon salt

¼ cup virgin olive oil

¼ teaspoon freshly ground black pepper

¼ teaspoon Tabasco sauce

1½ tablespoons Dijon-style mustard

1 tablespoon chopped parsley, or cilantro (fresh coriander or Chinese parsley)

3) Add the olive oil, remaining teaspoon of garlic, pepper, Tabasco, and mustard, and mix well. Set aside.

To cook patties:

1) Place the patties on a hot, well cleaned grill and cook for about 5 minutes on each side. Or, if a grill is not available, sauté the patties in a skillet over medium heat for about 5 minutes on each side.

2) To serve, divide the lentils among six plates and arrange two sausage patties on each plate. Sprinkle with the chopped parsley and serve immediately.

Yield: 6 servings

BRAISED PORK COCOTTE

In the interest of good health, it is important that you select a lean roast for this recipe. Although fatty roasts tend to be more moist, a lean one will be quite flavorful if it is cooked very slowly with its garnishes.

1   **lean pork loin roast (about 1½ lbs.)**

4   **cloves garlic, peeled and cut in half lengthwise**

½   **teaspoon salt**

¼   **teaspoon freshly ground black pepper**

1   **tablespoon virgin olive oil**

1   **large or 2 medium onions (8 oz.), peeled and quartered**

3   **carrots (8 oz.), peeled and cut into 1-inch pieces**

1   **tablespoon chopped fresh ginger**

1   **tablespoon chopped Jalapeño pepper**

½   **cup dried tomatoes reconstituted in 1 cup water (see Roasted Eggplant Sandwiches, page 118)**

1) Trim the pork roast of most of the surface fat and make eight random shallow slits in it. Push ½ a garlic clove in each of the slits. Sprinkle the roast with the salt and pepper.

2) Heat the oil in a cocotte (round or oval casserole dish) or heavy saucepan with lid. When hot, cook the pork for 10 minutes over high heat, turning the meat to brown it on all sides.

3) Add the onions, carrots, ginger, pepper and tomatoes, including the soaking water from the tomatoes.

4) Cover, reduce the heat to very, very low, and cook for about 1½ hours. The meat should be tender when pierced with a fork and there should be some juice surrounding it.

5) Serve two slices of the pork per person with the vegetable garnishes and juices.

Yield: 6 servings

· MAIN COURSE ·

SMOKED PORK ROAST WITH MUSTARD-HONEY GLAZE

Guests will love to help themselves to this flavorful glazed pork roast. Served with braised cabbage (page 98) and a simple salad, it makes a wonderful party menu.

1   **smoked picnic pork shoulder, bone in (about 6¼ lbs.)**

Glaze
2   **tablespoon honey**
2   **teaspoons dry mustard**
½   **teaspoon paprika**
⅛   **teaspoon cayenne pepper**

½   **cup water**
1   **tablespoon cider vinegar**

COOKING TECHNIQUE
Smoked pork shoulders, often called picnic hams, are available at most supermarkets. To enhance the taste of this "fully cooked" cut, re-cook it in water kept at about 180 to 190°; not only will the water draw salt from the meat, but it will make it substantially more moist and flavorful. Take care that the water doesn't exceed this 180° to 190° limit, however, or the ham may split open and actually lose moisture. It is important to trim away most of the fat, rind, and dark leathery skin from the meat after it is cooked; this gives it more eye-appeal and eliminates many of the calories.

1) Place the pork shoulder in a stock pot and cover it with enough cold water to extend ½-inch above the meat. Bring the water to 180° (this will take about 15 to 20 minutes) and cook at 180° to 190° for 1¼ hours. (Watch the temperature closely; the liquid should not boil.)

2) Meanwhile, in a small bowl mix together the honey, mustard, paprika and pepper. Set aside.

3) Let the pork cool in the cooking liquid, and then trim it, removing most of the exterior fat and rind from around the bones. Trim, also, the surface of the meat that is dark and leathery. Score the top of the ham every ¾-inch, and spread the glaze over the surface.

4) Place it in a roasting pan or saucepan and roast in a preheated 375° oven for 1 hour. The surface should be nicely browned.

5) Transfer the meat to a serving platter, and add the water and vinegar to the drippings in the pan. Using a wooden spatula, scrape the bottom of the pan to dissolve any solidified cooking juices, and mix them with the water and vinegar. Strain the juices over the pork shoulder, and serve, slicing it at the table.

Yield: 10 servings

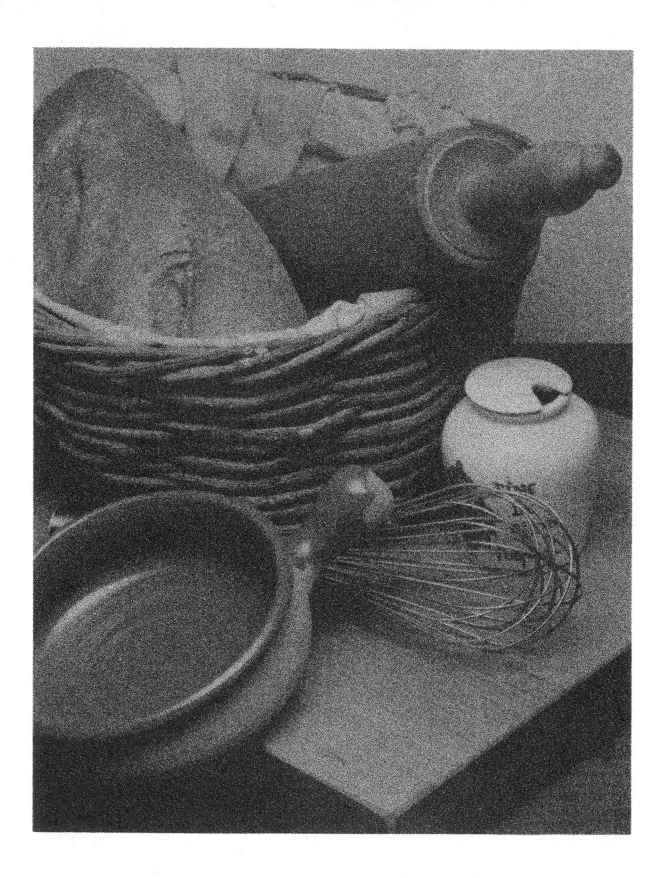

· ACCOMPANIMENTS ·

Tomato, Onion & Parsley Vinaigrette

Broccoli Piquante

Braised Sour Cabbage

Peas à la Française

Cauliflower in Scallion Sauce

Corn & Pepper Sauté

Carotte Ciboulette

Purée of Carrot with Ginger

Curried Bulgar with Currants

Cornmeal au Gruyère

Pommes Anglaises

French Fries

Pommes Persillade

Turnips & Mashed Potatoes

Oeuf Cocotte

Mushroom Omelet

Rolls & Baguettes

Buttermilk Bread

Croque-Monsieur

James Beard's Onion Sandwiches

Smoked Salmon & Cucumber Sandwiches

Roasted Eggplant Sandwiches

Olive & Tomato Toasts

Pan Bagna

Jam "Sandwiches"

TOMATO, ONION & PARSLEY VINAIGRETTE

This is especially good when tomatoes–preferably organically grown ones–are at their peak. The seasonings are simple, consisting only of vinegar, oil, salt, and pepper. If you don't have a red onion, you can use a mild Texas or Vidalia onion instead, and parsley can be replaced with basil, tarragon, or another herb to your liking. (Pictured on page 1.)

2   **large ripe tomatoes (about 1 lb.)**

1   **medium red onion (about 3 oz.)**

¼   **teaspoon salt**

¼   **teaspoon freshly ground black pepper**

1   **tablespoon red wine vinegar**

3   **tablespoons virgin olive oil**

2   **tablespoons chopped flat-leaf parsley**

1) Cut the tomatoes into ¼-inch slices and arrange the slices on a platter.

2) Peel the onion, cut it into very thin slices, and arrange on top of the tomato slices.

3) Sprinkle with salt, pepper, vinegar, and oil.

4) At serving time, sprinkle with parsley and serve.

Yield: 4 servings

BROCCOLI PIQUANTE

The broccoli is steamed briefly so it keeps all its nutrients and its deep green color. Flavored with a simple sauce made of lemon juice, olive oil, and Tabasco, this vegetable dish could be served as a first course. (Pictured on page 71.)

Sauce

1½ tablespoons lemon juice

2 tablespoons virgin olive oil

¼ teaspoon Tabasco sauce

¼ teaspoon salt

1½ pounds broccoli, cleaned

1) Combine the lemon juice, olive oil, Tabasco sauce and salt in a bowl. Mix well and set aside.

2) Separate the broccoli florets from the stems. Peel the stems, if the exterior is tough or fibrous, and cut them into slices about ½ inch thick by 2 inches long.

3) Arrange the broccoli florets and stems on an ovenproof plate and place in a steamer (mine is bamboo). Steam, covered, over boiling water for 11 to 12 minutes.

4) Toss gently with the sauce and serve.

Yield: 4 servings

BRAISED SOUR CABBAGE

The combination of sweet cider and cider vinegar gives this dish a sweet and sour taste that complements pork especially well, but also goes well with goose or duck. You can substitute red cabbage for Savoy cabbage and add some sliced apple, if you like.

1   pound Savoy cabbage, cored
     and cut into 1-inch slices
1   medium onion (about 6 oz.),
     peeled and sliced thin
¾   cup dark raisins
1   cup sweet cider
3   tablespoons cider vinegar
¾   teaspoon salt
¼   teaspoon freshly ground black
     pepper
½   tablespoon canola oil

1) In a stainless steel saucepan, combine the cabbage, onion, raisins, cider, cider vinegar, salt, pepper and oil.

2) Bring to a boil, cover, reduce the heat to medium, and boil for 45 minutes. Most of the liquid should have evaporated by then, but the cabbage should be moist; cook longer if there is excess moisture in the bottom of the pan. The small amount of liquid remaining in the pan should be caramelized and brown, and the cabbage a little crunchy. Serve.

Yield: 4 servings

PEAS A LA FRANCAISE

This is a classic dish. Boston lettuce and tiny pearl onions are cooked first with a dash of oil and water, and then fresh shelled peas are added; the mixture is cooked some more. If fresh peas are not available, a package of frozen baby peas will work quite well.

½ pound (about 24) small pearl onions

½ teaspoon herbes de Provence

1 tablespoon sugar

1 teaspoon salt

¼ teaspoon freshly ground black pepper

2 tablespoons virgin olive oil

1 cup water

1 small head (½ lb.) Boston lettuce, rinsed well and cut into 2-inch pieces

1½ pounds fresh peas shelled, or 1 package (12 oz.) frozen baby peas

1 teaspoon potato starch dissolved in 1 tablespoon water

1) In a saucepan combine the onions, herbes de Provence, sugar, salt, pepper, oil and water. Bring to a boil, reduce the heat, cover, and cook for 5 minutes. Add the lettuce and cook, covered, for about 3 to 4 minutes longer or until the lettuce has wilted. (The dish can be made ahead to this point.)

2) At serving time, add the peas to the lettuce mixture in the pan and bring to a boil. Boil for about 5 minutes if you are using fresh peas (adjusting as required based on the size of the peas), or 2 minutes if you are using frozen peas.

3) Mix in the dissolved potato starch solution and bring the mixture back to the boil to thicken the juices. Serve as soon as possible.

Yield: 4 servings

CAULIFLOWER IN SCALLION SAUCE

Crisp-tender cauliflower florets are served with a flavorful sauce of sautéed scallions. Lightly browned bread crumbs are sprinkled over the hot cauliflower at the last moment.

1	head cauliflower (about 1¼ lb), with greens removed
1	cup water
1	slice bread, toasted
3	tablespoons safflower oil
4	scallions, minced fine (½ cup)
¼	teaspoon salt
¼	teaspoon freshly ground black pepper

1) Separate the cauliflower into florets (making 14 to 16 pieces). In a large saucepan bring the water to a boil. Add the florets in one layer, cover, and boil over high heat for about 8 to 10 minutes or until tender. (Most of the water should have evaporated.)

2) Meanwhile, break the toasted bread into the bowl of a food processor and process it until crumbed. (You should have about 3 tbs.)

3) Heat the oil in a skillet. When hot, add the scallions and bread crumbs and sauté over medium heat for about 1½ minutes. Stir in the salt and pepper, and sprinkle the mixture over the hot cauliflower. Serve immediately.

Yield: 4 servings

PRESERVING NUTRIENTS
In this recipe, cauliflower florets are cooked in just enough water so that by the time the florets are tender, most of the water has evaporated and the nutrients and vitamins are preserved in the vegetable. If the dish is done ahead, reheat the cauliflower in a little water on top of the stove or in the oven.

· ACCOMPANIMENTS ·

CORN & PEPPER SAUTE

This is one of my favorite ways to prepare corn, high in Vitamins A and B, and red pepper, a good source of Vitamins A, B, C, and E . Fresh corn is sautéed very briefly in a skillet and, since the starch in it doesn't cook long enough to set, the corn remains crunchy and sweet. It's an easy dish, especially good if the corn comes from an organic farm. (Pictured on page 73.)

2   ears fresh corn
1   large red bell pepper (8 oz.)
2   tablespoons unsalted butter
¼   teaspoon salt
¼   teaspoon freshly ground black
     pepper

1) Husk the ears of corn and cut off the kernels, to make about 2 cups. Set aside.

2) Using a vegetable peeler, remove as much of the skin as you can from the red pepper. (The firmer the pepper, the easier it is to peel.) Cut the pepper into sections, remove the seeds from each section and peel off any remaining skin. Cut the pepper into ¼-inch pieces. (You should have about 1 cup.)

3) Heat the butter in a skillet. Add the corn and sauté in hot butter over high heat for about 2 minutes. Then add the red pepper, and sauté the mixture for 1½ minutes longer. Stir in the salt and pepper, and serve immediately.

Yield: 4 servings

PEELING PEPPERS
I peel the red pepper with a vegetable peeler for this recipe, instead of placing it under the broiler and peeling off the blistered skin, as is done conventionally. The vegetable remains quite firm and thick-walled when peeled. Use a good vegetable peeler and peel off as much of the skin from the whole vegetable as possible before cutting it into segments and removing additional skin from the recessed areas. Peeled pepper is quite sweet and is easily digested.

CAROTTE CIBOULETTE

These carrots are cooked in a little water along with butter and seasonings, but by the time they are cooked and tender, the water has evaporated, leaving all the nutrients and the concentrated taste of the seasoned carrots to enjoy.

1 pound carrots, peeled and sliced thin (about 3½ cups)
1 tablespoon unsalted butter
¾ cup water
1 teaspoon sugar
¾ teaspoon salt
¼ teaspoon freshly ground black pepper
2 tablespoons chopped chives, for garnish

1) Combine the carrots, butter, water, sugar, salt and pepper in a saucepan.

2) Bring to a boil, cover, and cook for 5 minutes, until most of the moisture has evaporated and the carrots are just tender. (If there is an excess amount of liquid remaining in the pan, cook, uncovered, for a few minutes, or until most of the liquid has evaporated and the carrots start sizzling.)

3) Sprinkle with the chives and serve as soon as possible.

Yield: 4 servings

PUREE OF CARROT WITH GINGER

The nutrient-rich water remaining in the saucepan after the carrots and ginger are cooked is added to the food processor to lend low-calorie moisture and flavor to the purée.

1½ pounds carrots, peeled
1 tablespoon peeled diced ginger
3 cups water
2 tablespoons virgin olive oil
¾ teaspoon salt
¼ teaspoon freshly ground black pepper
¼ cup milk

1) Cut the peeled carrots into 1½-inch chunks and place them in a saucepan. Add the ginger and water, and bring to a boil.

2) Cover the pan, reduce the heat and boil gently for 15 minutes, until tender. (Only about ½ cup of water should remain in the pan.)

3) Transfer the carrots and ginger with the cooking juices to the bowl of a food processor, and process for a few seconds and then add the remainder of the ingredients. Process until very smooth. Serve.

Yield: 4 servings (2½ cups)

CURRIED BULGAR WITH CURRANTS

Bulgar wheat–steamed, sun-dried and crushed wheat berries–is indigenous to Middle Eastern cooking. Like its uncooked relative, cracked wheat–another staple grain from that part of the world–it is high in protein, fiber, calcium, and potassium.

1   tablespoon virgin olive oil
1   small onion (2 oz.), chopped
2   scallions, coarsely chopped
    (about ¼ cup)
2   tablespoons dried currants
1   teaspoon curry powder
1   cup bulgar wheat (available
    at health food stores)
2   cups chicken stock, preferably
    homemade (see Chicken Broth,
    page 30)
½   teaspoon salt

1) In a skillet, heat the olive oil. When hot, add the onions and scallions, and sauté for 1 minute.

2) Stir in the currants and curry powder, then add the bulgar wheat, chicken stock, and salt. Mix well. Bring to a boil, cover, reduce the heat, and cook gently for 20 minutes. Fluff with a fork and serve immediately.

Yield: 4 servings

A WORD ABOUT BULGAR
You can make a salad with bulgar by simply reconstituting it in water and tossing it with vinegar, lemon juice, and seasonings–anything from scallions to garlic. Here, I cook the bulgar with onions, flavor it with curry and mix in some currants. A filling, high-carbohydrate dish that is quick, easy and inexpensive to make, it goes particularly well with Grilled Savory Lamb Chops (page 87).

CORNMEAL AU GRUYERE

Ready to eat in a few minutes, this fast polenta consists primarily of cornmeal and leeks, cooked together in a good chicken stock. If you want to lower the calories, serve this dish without the Gruyère cheese, although it adds texture and taste that go quite well with stews and roasted meat.

2¼ cups chicken stock, preferably homemade (see Chicken Broth, page 30)

1 piece of leek, trimmed and chopped fine (½ cup)

½ teaspoon salt

¼ teaspoon freshly ground black pepper

½ cup stone-ground yellow corn-meal

2 ounces Gruyère cheese, cut into ¼-inch dice (½ cup)

1) In a saucepan combine the stock, leek, salt, and pepper, and bring the mixture to a boil. Whisk in the cornmeal and return to the boil.

2) Lower the heat, cover, and cook gently for 4 to 5 minutes, stirring occasionally.

3) Add the cheese and mix until it has melted into the mixture. Serve immediately.

Yield: 4 servings

POMMES ANGLAISES

These are simply steamed potatoes. It is important that you use potatoes of approximately the same size for this dish. If you can't find small, round, red-skinned potatoes, cut larger potatoes into equal size chunks and round off the corners to make then more uniformly shaped. Prepared at the last moment and eaten freshly steamed, these are moist and delicate, much more so than potatoes cooked and left standing in water.

12 **small new potatoes (1½ lbs.), peeled**

1) Peel the potatoes and place them in a bowl of cold water until cooking time.

2) When ready to cook and serve, arrange them on an ovenproof plate and place in a steamer (mine is bamboo). Steam, covered, over boiling water for 26 minutes.

Yield: 4 servings

A LOW-CALORIE DINNER
For a complete low-calorie steamed dinner, serve the Pommes Anglaises with Salmon Pojarski (page 62) and Broccoli Piquante (page 97). I cook this menu in a three-tiered bamboo steamer, staggering the additions based on the cooking time required for each dish. I begin with the potatoes. Cover and steam them in one tier of the steamer over boiling water for 15 minutes. Then, a second tier containing broccoli is stacked on top, and the broccoli and potatoes steam, covered, for 5 additional minutes. Finally, the third tier is added, this one containing the salmon patties. Cover and steam all three tiers for an additional 6 to 7 minutes. Remove all three dishes from the steamer and serve together. Total steaming time for the meal is 26 minutes.

FRENCH FRIES

These French fries are cooked as they are in professional kitchens. First they are blanched in oil that is not too hot, thus allowing them to cook without taking on any color. This can be done hours ahead. Then, just before serving, they are browned quickly in very hot oil until crisp on the outside and soft and moist inside.

3   large Idaho or russet potatoes
    (2 lbs.)
1½ cups vegetable oil
    Salt to taste

1) Peel the potatoes and cut them lengthwise into sticks ½-inch thick. Wash the sticks in cold water, drain, and pat dry.

2) In a 12-inch non-stick skillet, heat the oil to 350°. Add the potatoes and cook for 5 minutes, until they are tender but still whitish. Remove and set aside until serving time. (You can prepare the recipe up to this point hours ahead.)

3) At serving time, reheat the oil to 400° and finish frying the potatoes, half at a time, for 4 to 5 minutes (shaking the pan occasionally to prevent then from sticking) until nicely browned and crisp.

4) Remove the potatoes from the oil, set them aside on absorbent paper, and repeat with the second batch. Sprinkle with salt and serve immediately.

Yield: 4 servings

A WORD ABOUT FRENCH FRIES
Notice that I start with 1½ cups of oil in this recipe. After the second cooking, you should have about 1¼ cups of oil remaining, meaning that the potatoes absorb only about ¼ cup of oil, or 1 table-spoon per portion. This is less oil than would have been used in the dressing if the potato had been made into a salad instead.

POMMES PERSILLADE

These potatoes are a standard item on most bistro menus. Cut into little cubes, they can be sautéed in just a few minutes. They are best served immediately after cooking; if cooked ahead, they soften and lose the exterior crispness that contrasts so well with their soft interior.

2   large potatoes (18 oz.), peeled
3   cloves garlic, peeled
¼   cup loosely packed parsley
     leaves
2   tablespoons canola oil
1   teaspoon salt
1   teaspoon freshly ground black
     pepper

1) Cut the potatoes into ⅜-inch cubes. Place in a sieve and rinse well under cool tap water. Place in a bowl with water to cover until ready to cook.

2) In a large non-stick skillet, heat the oil. Drain the potatoes, pat dry with paper towels and add to the hot oil. Sauté over high heat for 12 to 14 minutes, stirring occasionally, until the potatoes are browned on all sides.

3) Meanwhile, chop the garlic and parsley together until finely minced and set the mixture aside. (This is a *persillade.*) Add the salt, pepper and persillade to the potatoes in the skillet, tossing to combine. Serve immediately.

Yield: 4 servings

POTATOES IN ADVANCE
The potatoes can be peeled and cut into cubes ahead, providing they are kept in water to cover so they don't discolor. Drain, dry with paper towels, and sauté quickly just before serving in a little canola oil, which can withstand high temperatures.

TURNIPS AND MASHED POTATOES

In this recipe potatoes and turnips are cooked in just enough water so that there is about ½ cup of liquid remaining in the pan when the vegetables are tender–enough to incorporate with them to create a nice purée. If a little more liquid is required, add a dash of water or stock; if there is too much liquid in the pan after the vegetables are cooked, remove the lid and quickly boil to reduce the liquid to ½ cup.

3	large potatoes (18 oz.)
2	turnips (6 oz., total)
1	large clove garlic, peeled,
½	teaspoon salt
1	cup water
2	tablespoons unsalted butter

1) Peel the potatoes and turnips, and cut them into 2-inch pieces.

2) Place in a saucepan with the garlic, salt, and water. Bring to a boil, cover, reduce the heat, and boil gently for 20 minutes, until the vegetables are tender. There should be about ½ cup of liquid remaining. Adjust to this level, if necessary.

3) Transfer the mixture to the bowl of a food processor, add the butter and process until smooth and creamy. Serve.

Yield: 4 servings (2½ cups)

A HINT ABOUT FLAVOR
Although I don't use milk or cream, I do use a little butter. Select a good-quality butter and add it at the last moment for maximum taste advantage.

OEUF COCOTTE

These eggs are cooked in cocottes, which are little molds that hold about ½ cup. Although I use soufflé molds, you can use any small, ovenproof molds that are narrow enough so that an egg fills most of the container. The cocottes are then covered and cooked in a little boiling water, and, in my basic recipe, eaten directly from the molds.

2½ teaspoons unsalted butter
⅛ teaspoon salt
⅛ teaspoon freshly ground black pepper
4 large fresh eggs, preferably from free-range organic chickens
4 slices white bread

1) Butter the inside of four ½-cup soufflé molds with ½ teaspoon of the butter and sprinkle each lightly with the salt and pepper, dividing it evenly among the molds. Break one egg into each mold. In a large saucepan or high-sided skillet, bring ½ inch of water to a boil. Place the molds in the water and cover the pan with a lid. Boil gently for about 4 minutes, until the whites are set and the yolks still soft inside.

2) Meanwhile, toast the bread and spread one side of each slice with the remaining butter. Trim off the crusts, cut each slice into four thin rectangular strips, and serve with the molded eggs.

For variations:
1) Place 1 tablespoon of cooked peas in the bottom of a buttered mold and break the egg on top. Proceed as indicated above.

2) Sprinkle 1 tablespoon of chopped cooked ham around the yolk of a cooked egg and serve.

3) Press 2 teaspoons of minced green herbs (tarragon, chives, or chervil, for example) in the bottom and around the sides of a buttered mold. Break an egg into the mold and proceed as indicated above. To serve, run the blade of a sharp knife around the cooked egg and unmold it on a round crouton.

Yield: 4 servings

THREE VARIATIONS
There are three oeuf cocotte variations here: one with peas, one with ham, and one with herbs which are sprinkled on the bottom and sides of the greased molds before the eggs are added. This final variation is unmolded and served on a crouton. These eggs are an excellent vehicle for leftover meat or fish, which can be used as a garnish in the bottom of the molds. Sauce from a roast or fish dish also makes a nice addition here.

MUSHROOM OMELET

Omelet-making is a special technique that requires some practice, but the result is well worth the effort. This classic version made with three large fresh eggs, is garnished with thin slices of sautéed mushroom.

1   **large mushroom**
2   **teaspoons canola oil**
3   **large eggs, preferably from a free-range organic chicken**
     Dash salt
     Dash freshly ground black pepper
1   **teaspoon unsalted butter**

1) Cut the cap of the mushroom into slices and the stem into a dice. Heat the oil in a small skillet. When it is hot, add the sliced and diced mushroom pieces and sauté them in the oil for 45 seconds. Set aside. When cool enough to handle, arrange the mushroom slices in a row on the blade of a knife so they can be slid onto the top of the finished omelet for decoration.

2) In a bowl, beat the eggs with a fork and season them with the salt and pepper. Add the diced mushroom.

3) Heat the butter in an 8-inch non-stick skillet. Add the eggs and cook them over medium to high heat, stirring with one hand and vigorously shaking the pan with the other, until small, moist curds form. Stop stirring and allow the pan to sit on the heat for a few seconds, until a light skin forms on the underside of the omelet. Loosen the omelet around the edges and gently roll it so that both "lips" or edges join together.

4) Invert the omelet onto a plate and garnish it with the sliced mushrooms. Serve.

Yield: 1 omelet

A CLASSIC TECHNIQUE
This recipe demonstrates how to make a classic French omelet with soft, creamy curds. The idea here is to shake the pan with one hand while moving the flat base of a fork through the eggs with the other, so that the curds are very small. If the eggs are not mixed quickly enough, the curds harden. As soon as most of the mixture holds together, it is left for a few seconds so that enough of a skin can form on the underside of the omelet that it can be rolled together and inverted onto a plate.

ROLLS & BAGUETTES

Made in a food processor, these rolls and baguettes are quick to make, thick, and crusty. Smart cooks know that the secret of any good-tasting sandwich is the bread. This easy-to-bake recipe for an all-purpose bread dough is used in preparing any number of sandwiches. When baked as a

2   envelopes yeast

2   cups tepid water from the tap (about 110°)

½   teaspoon sugar

4½ cups bread flour (1 lb., 5 oz.)

1   cup rolled wheat (3 oz.)

1½ teaspoons salt

1   to 2 teaspoons peanut oil

1   tablespoon yellow cornmeal

1   teaspoon all-purpose flour

1) Place the yeast, water and sugar in the bowl of a food processor and let proof for 5 minutes. Add the bread flour, rolled wheat, and salt to the processor bowl and process for 1 to 2 minutes, until the ingredients form into a ball. Grease a bowl with half the peanut oil and place the dough in the bowl. Cover with plastic wrap and let proof at room temperature for 1½ to 2 hours, until double or triple in bulk.

2) Push down gently on the proofed dough to let the air out. Place it on a large cookie sheet and, using your hands, spread it out to a rectangle about 14 by 9 inches, oiling your hands lightly if the dough sticks. Cut the rectangle into four strips, then move two strips to one side of the sheet, and sprinkle them on both sides with half the cornmeal. They should be extended the length of the sheet into two baguettes.

3) Cut each of the two remaining strips into three rectangles. Arrange these next to the uncut strips and sprinkle them on both sides with the remaining cornmeal.

4) Oil the loaves and rolls lightly on top with the remaining peanut oil and cover them gently with a sheet of plastic wrap. The oil will prevent the plastic wrap from sticking to the loaves when it is removed after proofing. The plastic wrap prevents the dough from drying out and crusting on top.

A WORD ABOUT DOUGH
Depending on where in the country you live and the temperature and humidity at the time of year when you bake the bread, the quantity of yeast may need adjusting. If the weather is particularly humid, for example, 1½ envelopes of yeast may be sufficient for 4½ cups of flour. Be sure to dip your measuring cup directly into the flour and then level it off to get the proper amount of flour, which is 1 pound, 5 ounces for 4½ cups.

baguette, it can be thinly sliced, spread with a delicious tomato mixture and then quickly broiled, as in Olive & Tomato Toasts (page 119). Or, when shaped and then baked as a large loaf, it can be hollowed out and filled with meat and vegetables, as in Pan Bagna (page 120).

5) Let the loaves and rolls proof for 45 minutes to 1 hour, until double in bulk. Sprinkle the tops with the teaspoon of flour. Make a lengthwise slash or criss-cross slashes down the center of each loaf and roll with a razor blade.

6) Place in a preheated 450° oven and immediately throw 2 tablespoons of water onto the oven floor and close the oven door quickly. This produces steam, which helps create bread with a crustier exterior. Repeat this procedure 5 minutes later.

7) Bake the loaves and rolls for a total of 22 to 25 minutes (checking them after 15 minutes and placing another tray under them if they are browning too quickly). Remove from the oven when they are dark brown and sound hollow when tapped with a spoon or knife. Cool on a rack.

Yield: 2 baguettes and 6 rolls

BROWN & SERVE TECHNIQUE
At home, I often partially bake rolls and baguettes, removing them from the oven after 12 to 15 minutes, when they have achieved maximum size, but are not yet brown. Let the loaves cool until lukewarm, wrap tightly, and freeze. When needed, unwrap the frozen bread and place it directly on the center rack of a preheated 400° oven. Bake for 15 minutes, until brown and crusty.

BUTTERMILK BREAD

This bread is very dense and freezes well, although it will keep a few days without freezing. Cut into very thin slices, it is ideal for breakfast with the Smoked Whitefish Mold (page 49), but also goes well with caviar, smoked salmon or the like.

1   envelope yeast
½   cup tepid water from the tap (about 110°)
1   tablespoon sugar
½   stick (2 oz.) unsalted butter
2   cups (about 10 oz.) whole wheat flour
2   cups (about 10 oz.) bread flour
1   cup buttermilk, plus additional for brushing on the loaf before baking
1   teaspoon salt
½   teaspoon canola oil

1) Place the yeast, water and sugar in the bowl of a food processor and allow to proof for 10 minutes. Add the butter, wholewheat flour, bread flour, buttermilk and salt, and process for 1 minute. Oil a large bowl, and place the dough in the bowl. Set aside to proof, covered, for 2 hours.

2) Punch the dough down into the bowl and shape it into a ball about 6 inches in diameter. Place the ball of dough on a cookie sheet and cover with the overturned proofing bowl. Allow to proof for 1 hour more.

3) Brush the proofed dough with the additional buttermilk. Using a razor blade, make a crisscross slash on the top of the round loaf. Place in a preheated 400° oven for 45 to 50 minutes, until hollow sounding when tapped. Cool to room temperature, slice and serve.

Yield: 8 to 10 servings

CROQUE-MONSIEUR

The *croque-monsieur* is a classic toasted ham and cheese sandwich. I make it here with Gruyère cheese, as is traditional in France. Cut into little squares as it emerges from the oven, it makes a terrific hot hors d'oeuvre. You can vary it–for a *croque-madame*, for example, replace the ham with a slice of chicken.

2   **tablespoons canola oil**
8   **slices white bread (6 oz.)**
8   **slices Gruyère cheese (about 4 oz.)**
4   **slices honey-cured ham (4 oz.)**

1) Grease a cookie sheet with the oil. Dip the bread slices (on one side only) in the oil, and arrange them, oiled side up, on the table.

2) Place a slice of cheese on top of each slice of bread. Arrange a slice of ham on four of the cheese-covered bread slices, invert the remaining cheese-covered bread slices on top and press together.

3) Dip both sides of the sandwiches in the remaining oil on the tray, and place the tray in a preheated 400° oven for 10 minutes.

4) To serve, trim the crusts from the bread and cut the sandwiches diagonally into triangles. Serve hot.

Yield: 4 servings

JAMES BEARD'S ONION SANDWICHES

I first tasted this great combination when I went to see James Beard one Sunday morning in the mid-60's. Ever since, these onion sandwiches have been a favorite at my house. Rolled on its edge in mayonnaise and then in minced chives, the sandwich is as attractive as it is delicious. (Pictured on page 159.)

- 8 thin slices white bread (8 oz.)
- 6 tablespoons mayonnaise
- 4 teaspoons Dijon-style mustard
- 4 slices red onion, cut 1 inch thick from an onion about 3½ inches in diameter
- 4 tablespoons finely minced chives

1) Arrange the bread slices next to one another on a flat work surface and, using a glass or a round cutter, cut circles as large as possible out of the slices.

2) Spread each bread circle with 1 teaspoon of the mayonnaise and then with ½ teaspoon of the mustard. Place an onion slice on four of the bread discs (it should cover to the edge). Top with the remaining bread circles. Press lightly to make them adhere.

3) Spread remaining mayonnaise on the outside edge of each sandwich (about 2 teaspoons per sandwich), and then roll the edge in the chives until coated. Press lightly to make them adhere. Serve.

Yield: 4 servings

SMOKED SALMON & CUCUMBER SANDWICHES

M̲ade with smoked salmon and a delicious cucumber relish, this sandwich can be assembled in just a few minutes. (Pictured on page 159.)

Cucumber Relish

⅔ cup hot water

⅓ cup white distilled vinegar

½ teaspoon salt

½ teaspoon sugar

1 cucumber (12 oz.), peeled, seeded and sliced crosswise very thin

1 shallot, peeled and sliced very thin (2 tbs.)

1½ teaspoons finely minced Jalapeño pepper

2 tablespoons chopped cilantro leaves

8 slices white bread

6 slices smoked salmon (about 8 oz. total)

1) In a bowl combine the hot water, vinegar, salt, and sugar. Stir in the cucumbers, shallots, Jalapeño pepper and cilantro. Allow the mixture to macerate for at least one hour before using, or cover and keep for up to 2 weeks in the refrigerator.

2) At serving time, toast the bread. Drain the cucumbers and arrange half of them on 4 slices of toasted bread. Place the salmon slices on top of the cucumbers; top with remaining cucumbers.

3) Arrange the remaining pieces of toast on top and trim off the crusts. Cut each sandwich in half to create 2 rectangles and serve immediately.

Yield: 4 servings

CUCUMBER RELISH
This simple, fresh-tasting relish has become a standard ingredient at my house. It keeps for weeks in the refrigerator and is delicious on any sandwich and as an accompaniment to grilled meat or fish. The use of the relish here eliminates the need for butter or mayonnaise, making for a lighter, more savory sandwich.

ROASTED EGGPLANT SANDWICHES

Eggplant sandwiches are different and delicious. They feature thin slices of sautéed eggplant layered with dried tomatoes, fresh basil and mozzarella cheese on a homemade French roll. (Pictured on page 159.)

1   cup dried (**not** reconstituted) tomatoes (about 1½ oz.)
1   tablespoon virgin olive oil
¼   cup canola oil
1   eggplant (about 1 lb.), cut into 16 slices, each about ⅜-inch thick
    Salt and freshly ground pepper to taste
4   oval rolls (see Rolls & Baguettes, page 112)
4   ounces mozzarella cheese, sliced thin or grated
12 large basil leaves

1) In a saucepan, bring 1½ cups of water to a boil. Add the dried tomatoes and soak for about 10 minutes. Drain (reserving the liquid for stock) and mix the tomatoes with the olive oil.

2) Heat 1 tablespoon of the canola oil in each of two non-stick skillets and when hot, place 4 slices of eggplant in each skillet. Sprinkle with salt and pepper and cook 5 minutes on each side over medium heat. Remove to a dish and repeat with the remaining oil and eggplant.

3) Split the rolls in half and place them, cut side up, on the table. Place 2 slices of eggplant on the bottom half of each roll. Divide the reconstituted tomato halves on top of the eggplant and arrange 3 basil leaves on top. Cover with 3 thin slices (or grated equivalent) of cheese. Sprinkle, if desired, with a little salt and pepper, and add the remaining eggplant slices, 2 per roll. Put the top half of the rolls in place and arrange the assembled sandwiches on a tray.

4) Bake in a preheated 400° oven for 10 to 12 minutes, until the cheese inside is completely melted. Cut into halves and serve.

Yield: 4 sandwiches

DRIED TOMATOES
This recipe makes use of dried tomatoes that you reconstitute yourself quite inexpensively (as opposed to buying the costly commercially reconstituted tomatoes in oil). After soaking the tomatoes in boiling water, transfer them to a jar and mix in a little olive oil. To create a concoction of your own, add whatever garnishes you like–from sliced garlic to sprigs of rosemary, pieces of walnuts or hazelnuts, or hot peppers. Use this mixture on pasta as well as on sandwiches.

OLIVE & TOMATO TOASTS

These "toasts"–either baked and served hot from the oven or unbaked and served at room temperature–are great to pass around at large parties. The fresh tomatoes, cut into little cubes, have a sweet taste that goes so well with the concentrated taste of the oil-cured black olives. (Pictured on page 159.)

4   tablespoons virgin olive oil

16 slices from a baguette, cut ½-inch thick

2   tomatoes, seeded and cut into ¼-inch dice (1⅓ cups)

½   cup oil-cured black olives, pitted and cut into ¼-inch pieces

4   tablespoons minced cilantro (also called fresh coriander or Chinese parsley)

½   teaspoon freshly ground black pepper

¼   teaspoon salt

1½ tablespoons grated Parmesan cheese

1) Spread 2 tablespoons of the olive oil on a cookie sheet and dip both sides of the bread slices in the oil. Arrange on the sheet and bake in a preheated 400° oven for 6 to 8 minutes, until lightly browned. Remove from oven and set aside.

2) Meanwhile, in a bowl combine the tomatoes, olives, remaining 2 tablespoons olive oil, cilantro, pepper and salt.

3) Divide and spread the mixture evenly on top of each piece of toast. Sprinkle with grated cheese.

4) Return to the 400° oven for 5 minutes and serve warm, or serve unbaked at room temperature.

Yield: 4 servings

PAN BAGNA

This light, healthy picnic sandwich is especially good when made ahead–preferably the day before–on a large round bread loaf.

½ cucumber (about 7 oz.)

1 round crusty country-style loaf of bread (about 1 lb.)

18 black oil-cured olives, pitted and chopped

3 cloves garlic, peeled, crushed, and finely chopped

10 small anchovy fillets, coarsely chopped (2 oz. can)

2 tablespoons virgin olive oil

4 to 5 thin slices of red onion

⅓ green bell pepper (2 oz.), seeded and sliced thin

1 ripe tomato, sliced thin

¼ teaspoon salt

¼ teaspoon freshly ground black pepper

12 large basil leaves

BATHED BREAD
Pan Bagna literally means "bathed bread." It originally consisted of a salad of different vegetables–from tomatoes to onions, red pepper, and garlic–that were mixed with pieces of leftover bread so that the bread was soaked with vegetable juices. In the more modern version, salad ingredients are placed in a split loaf of bread. The loaf is then wrapped and weighted down. The juices flow through the bread and the filling becomes compact enough so that the loaf can be cut into pieces.

1) Peel the cucumber and slice it lengthwise with a vegetable peeler into long thin strips, discarding the seedy center.

2) Cut the loaf of bread in half horizontally.

3) In a bowl mix together the olives, garlic, anchovies (with their oil) and olive oil. Spread the mixture on the cut surface of both bread halves, then arrange the slices of onion, green pepper and tomato on the bottom half of the loaf. Sprinkle with salt and pepper, arrange the basil leaves and then the cucumber slices on top.

4) Invert the top half of the bread to reform the loaf and wrap it tightly in plastic wrap. Refrigerate for 2 to 3 hours with a 5-pound weight on top (canned goods or a milk carton).This enables the juices in the filling to flow through the bread.

5) At serving time, unwrap the loaf and cut it into wedges to serve.

Yield: 4 servings

JAM "SANDWICHES"

Jam sandwiches are fun to make for a party. Consisting of thin slices of firm-textured pound cake spread with different flavored jams, these can be served stacked up together in traditional "sandwich" fashion, or they can be served open-face, with a colorful jam spread on the surface of each cake slice. To add diversity to a dessert tray, select the flavors to suit your own tastes, cutting each one into a different shape.

6   ounces fine-textured pound
    cake

1½ tablespoons raspberry jam

1½ tablespoons apricot jam

1½ tablespoons strawberry jam

Note:
    The piece of pound cake I used
    was 6-inches long by 5-inches
    wide

1) Trim the outside of the pound cake and cut it into six slices, each ¼-inch thick. Spread the raspberry jam on the top surface of one slice, the apricot jam on the top surface of another slice, and the strawberry jam on the top surface of a third slice.

2) Top with the remaining pound cake slices to create three "sandwiches." Cut each "sandwich" into different shapes: one into squares, one into triangles, and one into rectangles.

3) Arrange on a plate and serve.

Yield: 4 servings

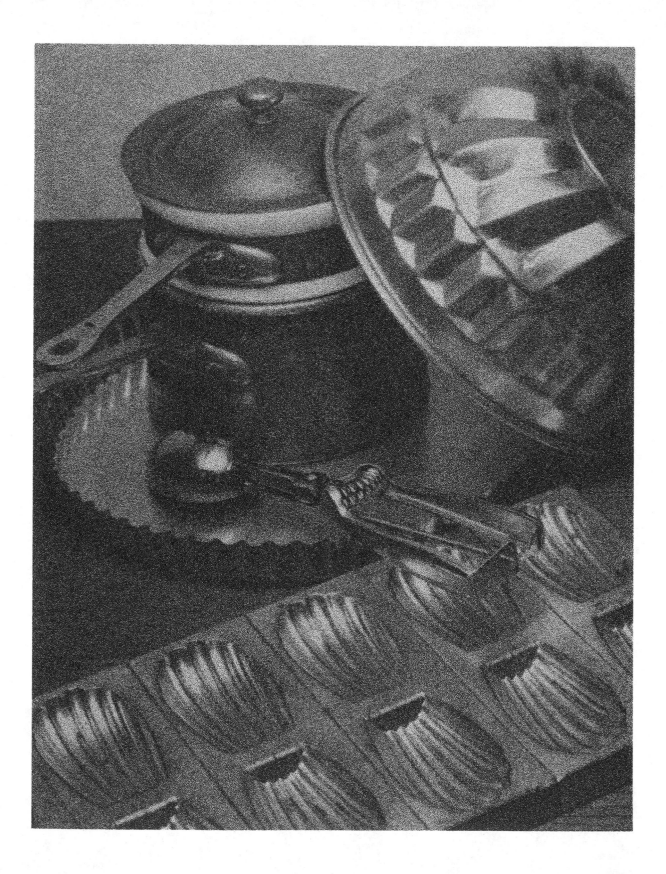

· DESSERTS ·

Almond Cake with Mango Coulis
Baked Apple Tart
Caramelized Apple Timbales
Baked Apricots with Almonds
Baked Bananas in Lemon-Rum Sauce
Blueberries with Brown Sugar
Cherry Bread Pudding
Chocolate & Fruit Nut Cups
Chocolate Mint Truffles
Chocolate Soufflé Cake with Raspberry-Rum Sauce
Coffee Creme Caramel
Orange & Grapefruit Segments
Figs Villamora
Calimyrna Figs in Spicy Port Sauce
Fresh Fruit with Minted Apricot Fondue
Grapes & Raisins in Lime Cookie Cones
Hazelnut Parfait with Candied Violets
Oranges in Grand Marnier
Crepes Soufflés in Grapefruit Sauce
Salpicon of Pineapple
Baked Pears with Figs
Pistachio Floating Island with Blackcurrant Sauce
Raspberry Granité
Strawberry Buttermilk Shortcakes
Candied Orange Rind

ALMOND CAKE WITH MANGO COULIS

Colorful mango *coulis*, flavored with rum and a bit of honey, is the perfect accompaniment to my favorite almond cake. Be sure to only use very ripe mangoes! For a more festive presentation, sprinkle additional sliced almonds on the batter just before baking. (Pictured on page 139.)

1	tablespoon plus ½ teaspoon canola oil
5½	ounces sliced almonds (1½ cups)
¾	cup granulated sugar
¼	cup potato starch
1	tablespoon unsalted butter, softened
1	teaspoon vanilla extract
3	egg yolks
2	tablespoons milk
5	egg whites

Mango Coulis

1	ripe mango (about 1 lb.)
¼	cup water
2	tablespoons dark rum
1	tablespoon lemon juice
2	tablespoons honey

CAKE TECHNIQUES

To make this traditional cake less caloric, I have drastically reduced the amount of butter and the number of egg yolks. Be sure that the egg whites are beaten until fairly firm, and that they are folded into the almond batter quickly enough so they don't have a chance to deflate. Folding should take only a few seconds with a spatula. Transfer to the greased baking mold and bake immediately in the oven.

1) Preheat oven to 325°. Grease the bottom and sides of a 8 by 1-inch mold with ½ teaspoon vegetable oil and line the bottom of the mold with parchment paper.

2) In the bowl of a food processor, place the almonds, ¼ cup of the sugar and the potato starch. Process until the nuts are finely ground. Add the butter, remaining oil, all but two tablepoons of the sugar, vanilla, egg yolks and milk and process just until the mixture is smooth. Transfer it to a bowl.

3) In another bowl, beat the egg whites until firm, then add the reserved 2 tablespoons of sugar and beat for a few seconds longer.

4) Fold the egg white mixture into the almond mixture and transfer the batter to the greased mold. Bake in the preheated oven for 35 minutes, or until set. Cool on a rack.

For mango coulis:

1) Cut the mango in half lengthwise and scoop out the flesh. Place the flesh in the bowl of a food processor and process until smooth. Add the water, rum, lemon juice and honey and process until smooth.

2) To serve, unmold the cake, cut it into wedges, and serve it with the mango coulis.

Yield: 10 servings

BAKED APPLE TART

Cored, halved apples filled with apricot jam are wrapped in a round of pastry dough and dusted with a sprinkling of sugar before baking. I prefer serving this tart at room temperature. (Pictured on page 140.)

Dough
- ¾ cup all-purpose flour (3 oz.)
- 3 tablespoon unsalted butter, cold
- ½ teaspoon granulated sugar
- 2 tablespoons water, ice cold

Filling
- 2 large Golden Delicious apples (1 lb.)
- 2 tablespoons apricot jam
- 1 tablespoon granulated sugar
- ½ tablespoon unsalted butter

CLASSIC DOUGH
The classic dough for this dessert is suitable for most baking needs and is easily made in a food processor. It is important that you not overmix the ingredients, however. The butter should not be totally incorporated into the flour; visible pieces will melt as the dough cooks and it will develop some of the flakiness evident in puff pastry. Notice that there is no waste; the dough is rolled free-form on a cookie sheet and the edges folded back over the apples, so trimming is not required, as it would be if the tart were made in a conventional pie plate.

For dough:

1) Preheat oven to 400°.

2) In the bowl of a food processor, place the flour, butter (cut into ½-inch pieces) and sugar. Process for 5 seconds, and then add the water and process for another 5 seconds. Remove the dough, even if not compactly mixed, and press it between two layers of plastic wrap. Roll it out to form a circle about 10 inches in diameter. Transfer to a cookie sheet and refrigerate.

For filling:

1) Meanwhile, peel the apples and cut them in half. Remove the cores and hollow them out a little with a measuring spoon. Chop the trimmings obtained from hollowing out the fruit (you should have about ¾ cup). Place ½ tablespoon jam in the hollow of each apple half and arrange the halves, cut side down, in the center of the circle of dough. Sprinkle the chopped apple around the halves.

2) Bring the edge of the dough up over the apples to create a border, 1 to 2 inches high, around the edge. (This will create a receptacle that will hold the cooking juices inside.)

3) Sprinkle the top of the tart with sugar and dot with butter. Bake in the preheated oven for 45 minutes to 1 hour, until well browned and crusty. Serve warm or at room temperature.

Yield: 4 servings

CARAMELIZED APPLE TIMBALES

This dessert is easy to make ahead. Arrange the cooked, caramelized apples in tiny, plastic-lined soufflé molds so they are easy to unmold. Notice that the apples are not peeled; the skin gives some chewiness and texture to the dish. The concentrated taste is particularly pleasing when the timbales are served with a little sour cream or plain yogurt.

4	large Golden Delicious apples (about 1½ lbs.)
2	teaspoons julienned lemon rind
4	tablespoons granulated sugar
3	tablespoons water plus ⅓ cup water
2	tablespoons lemon juice
1	tablespoon unsalted butter
4	tablespoons sour cream or yogurt

1) Remove the apple stems with a little adjoining skin and flesh and place them in a bowl with lemon juice. Set aside for use as a decoration.

2) Cut the apples in half lengthwise and core them. Then cut each half crosswise into ¼ inch thick slices to make about 6 loosely packed cups.

3) In a skillet, combine the sugar and 3 tablespoons water and cook over medium high heat until the mixture turns into a dark brown caramel (about 3 to 4 minutes). Add the apple slices, the lemon rind, ⅓ cup water and butter. Mix well, reduce the heat, and cook at a gentle boil, covered, for about 7 minutes. (The apples should be tender and most of the moisture gone.) Remove the lid and cook, rolling the apples in the caramel, for about 5 minutes over high heat until the juice has turned again into caramel and the apple pieces are browned. Let cool to lukewarm.

4) Meanwhile, line four small soufflé molds or ramekins (about ½ to ¾-cup capacity) with plastic wrap. Pack the lukewarm apple mixture into the molds, cover with plastic wrap and refrigerate until cold.

5) At serving time, unmold the timbales and decorate them with the reserved apple stems. Serve with a tablespoon of sour cream or yogurt.

Yield: 4 servings

BAKED APRICOTS WITH ALMONDS

The success of this dish depends on the quality of the apricots you use. If you have very ripe, full-flavored fruit, preferably from an organic farm, you will have terrific results. I used to make this dessert with a lot of heavy cream; now I use just a little half-and-half. If you want to go one step further, eliminate the half-and-half and add a few tablespoons of water to lend a little moisture to the fruit.

1   **pound ripe apricots (about 6 or 7)**

3   **tablespoons apricot jam**

¼   **cup half-and-half**

2   **tablespoons sliced almonds**

1   **tablespoon granulated sugar**

1) Preheat oven to 350°.

2) Cut the apricots in half and remove their pits.

3) Arrange the apricot halves, cut side down, in a gratin dish. Spoon the jam over the fruit, and pour the half-and-half around the fruit. Sprinkle the almonds and sugar on top.

4) Place in the preheated oven for 30 to 35 minutes. Serve lukewarm or at room temperature.

Yield: 6 servings

BAKED BANANAS IN LEMON-RUM SAUCE

Bananas are almost nature's perfect food–high in potassium, calcium, and Vitamins A, B, and C. Available year round, they are best when little black spots begin to form on the skin, indicating they are very ripe. You will notice that the skin blackens completely after 15 minutes of cooking. At that point, you can remove the fruit and simply serve it with a little lemon juice or with the tart lemon-rum sauce below.

4   very ripe bananas, with black-spotted skin (about 2 lbs.)

Lemon-Rum Sauce
1   tablespoon grated lemon rind
2   tablespoons lemon juice
2   tablespoons granulated sugar
3   tablespoons orange marmalade
¼   cup water

2   tablespoons dark rum
    Mint leaves, for garnish
    Strips of orange peel, for garnish

1) Preheat oven to 400°.

2) Trim the ends of the bananas, removing about ½-inch from each end, and cut a slit through the skin extending the length of the fruit. Arrange the unpeeled bananas on a cookie sheet and place in the preheated oven for 15 minutes. (The skin will turn black.)

3) Meanwhile, in a saucepan mix together the lemon rind, lemon juice, sugar, marmalade and water and bring the mixture to a boil. Boil for 1 minute, then transfer to a serving dish.

4) As soon as the bananas are cool enough to handle, remove the skin and place them in the sauce. Using a spoon, coat the bananas on all sides with the sauce.

5) When cool, stir in the rum and decorate the bananas with mint leaves and orange peel. Serve.

Yield: 4 servings

BLUEBERRIES WITH BROWN SUGAR

This is a simple, delicious summer recipe. Look over the blueberries carefully and remove and discard any damaged ones. If you wash them, dry then off with paper towels so the water doesn't dilute the yogurt. The best way to serve the berries is to arrange them on individual plates, create a well in the center, and then spoon the yogurt into the well and sprinkle it with the brown sugar. If you desire a richer dessert, substitute sour cream or whipped cream for the yogurt, and sprinkle it with brown sugar.

1   **pint blueberries**
8   **tablespoons plain yogurt**
4   **tablespoons dark brown sugar**
    Mint leaves, for garnish

1) Divide the blueberries among four plates. Make a well in the center of the berries and spoon in some yogurt.

2) Sprinkle the berries and yogurt with the brown sugar, decorate with a few mint leaves, and serve.

Note:
The sugar will melt and spread somewhat on the yogurt, giving the dessert an interesting look.

Yield: 4 servings

CHERRY BREAD PUDDING

This is a great dessert to make when Bing cherries are in full season. You can make the same recipe with berries or pieces of plum instead of cherries. Flavor them with the almond-sugar mixture, too. This dessert is best served lukewarm with a little sour cream or, if you prefer, yogurt.

1	**pound ripe cherries (14 oz. pitted)**
3	**slices white bread, toasted**
1	**cup milk**
½	**cup sliced almonds, toasted**
½	**cup cherry preserves**
1	**teaspoon unsalted butter**
4	**teaspoons granulated sugar**
½	**teaspoon confectioners' sugar**
1	**cup sour cream or yogurt**

1) Preheat oven to 350°.

2) Pit the cherries. Then coarsely crumble the toasted bread (you should have 1 cup) and place it in a bowl with the milk. Mix well, and add the cherries, toasted almonds (reserving 2 tbs.) and the cherry preserves.

3) In another bowl, mix the reserved almonds with 2 teaspoons of the sugar.

4) Grease a 6-cup gratin dish with the butter and sprinkle it with the remaining 2 teaspoons of sugar. Pour the cherry mixture into the dish and top with the almond-sugar mixture.

5) Bake in the preheated oven for 35 to 40 minutes. Cool to lukewarm, sprinkle with confectioners' sugar and serve with sour cream, if desired.

Yield: 6 servings

CHOCOLATE & FRUIT NUT CUPS

These "cups" are more a candy or petit-four than a dessert. They are especially fun to make with children, who love to select their own assortment of fruits and nuts and press them into the soft chocolate. The result is beautiful and delicious and if you can refrain from eating more than two of them, the calorie intake is not too frightening. (Pictured on page 160.)

4	ounces bittersweet chocolate
1	tablespoon sliced almonds
1	tablespoon pecan pieces
1	tablespoon pumpkin seeds
1	tablespoon golden raisins
1	tablespoon Muscat raisins
1	large strawberry, cut into 12 wedges
3	mint leaves, cut in pieces
12	small midget-size foil or paper cups (1½-inch diameter by 1-inch deep)

1) Melt the chocolate in a double boiler or in a microwave oven. (You should have about ⅓ cup of melted chocolate.) Divide the melted chocolate among the 12 cups, filling the base of each with about ¼ inch of chocolate.

2) While the chocolate is still liquid, arrange the nuts, pumpkin seeds, raisins, strawberry wedges and mint leaves on top and press on them lightly to partially imbed them in the chocolate. Refrigerate for about 1 hour, until hardened.

3) To serve, remove the "cups" from their foil or paper casing, arrange then on a plate and pass for dessert.

Yield: 6 servings

CHOCOLATE MINT TRUFFLES

There are about 30 calories in each of these small truffles, not as many as you might expect, considering their rich flavor. These are especially nice to box and give to friends over the holiday season. They keep well in the refrigerator and can also be frozen. (Pictured on page 160.)

¼ pound bittersweet chocolate

2 tablespoons milk

1 egg yolk

2 teaspoons finely minced mint

2 teaspoons unsweetened cocoa powder

1) Place the chocolate and milk together, either in a double boiler over hot water, or in a microwave oven set at medium level for 30 seconds at a time. Heat until the chocolate has melted.

2) Stir to combine, then add the egg yolk and mint, and mix well. (At this point, the mixture can be heated in a double boiler to 140° and held at that temperature for 3 to 4 minutes to kill any possible salmonella bacteria in the egg yolk.)

3) Cool the mixture to room temperature and then cover and refrigerate it for at least 1 hour until firm.

4) Divide the cold chocolate mixture into 20 small pieces and press each piece into a roundish ball. (The balls should be uneven so they look more like real truffles.) Sprinkle cocoa over the balls on the plate, shaking the plate so the truffles roll around in the cocoa and become coated.

5) Transfer the truffles to a clean plate and refrigerate them until serving time.

Yield: 20 small truffles

CHOCOLATE SOUFFLE CAKE WITH RASPBERRY-RUM SAUCE

This light cake containing fewer egg yolks and less starch and butter than is customary for this type of dessert, is fluffy and delicate. Serve at room temperature, with or without the sauce. (Pictured on page 141.)

2 tablespoons plus 1 teaspoon canola oil

6 ounces dark bittersweet chocolate

¼ cup (½ stick) unsalted butter or butter substitute

¼ cup granulated sugar

2 tablespoons potato starch

2 egg yolks

6 egg whites

½ teaspoon confectioners' sugar

Raspberry-Rum Sauce

½ cup raspberry preserves (preferably seedless)

1 tablespoon dark rum

1) Preheat oven to 325°.

2) Grease a round cake mold measuring 9 inches across and 3 inches deep with 1 teaspoon oil.

3) Combine the chocolate, butter, 2 tablespoons remaining oil and sugar in the top of a double boiler (or in a microwave-safe bowl). Cook over boiling water (or in a microwave) until the chocolate and butter have melted. Stir to combine. Add the potato starch and mix it in with a whisk. Then whisk in the egg yolks; the mixture will thicken.

4) Whip egg whites until firm and fold them lightly and as quickly as possible into the chocolate mixture. Pour the batter into the mold and place it in the preheated oven for about 30 minutes. The cake should still be a little soft in the center.

5) Let cool to lukewarm. Invert onto a plate, and then invert back onto a serving platter. Sprinkle with confectioners' sugar.

For sauce:
1) In a bowl, combine the raspberry preserves (straining them first if using preserves with seeds) with the rum and 1 tablespoon of water.

2) To serve, arrange a slice of cake on each dessert dish and spoon some sauce alongside.

Yield: 6 to 8 servings

COFFEE CREME CARAMEL

You can make the caramel for this light, flavorful dessert in a separate pan, but it simplifies the preparation if you make it right in the casserole dish where you make the dessert. Keep a pan of cold water handy, however, and dip the base of the casserole in the water if the caramel continues to cook and darken after it is removed from the heat. If you prepare the caramel in a separate pan, add additional sugar to accommodate the amount of caramel lost when you transfer it to the casserole.

Caramel

2	tablespoons sugar
1	tablespoon water

1½	cups milk
2	tablespoons granulated sugar
1	tablespoon instant expresso coffee
1	egg
1	egg white

1) Preheat oven to 350°.

2) In a 2-cup ceramic or metal casserole that can be used over direct heat, combine the sugar and water and cook over medium heat until caramelized, about 4 to 5 minutes. Set aside.

3) In a saucepan, combine the milk, sugar and coffee. Warm the mixture just enough to melt the instant coffee. Whisk in the whole egg and egg white. Pour mixture through a strainer over the caramel.

4) Set the casserole dish in a larger pan and surround it with warm tap water. Place in the preheated oven and bake for 50 to 60 minutes, until set, checking from time to time to make sure the water does not boil. (If it does, add a few ice cubes to cool it to below the boil.)

5) Cool for at least 4 hours and then unmold to serve.

Yield: 4 servings

ORANGE & GRAPEFRUIT SEGMENTS

This is an attractive dish, especially if you use blood oranges, which contrast nicely with the grapefruit. In addition to using the flesh of the oranges and grapefruits, I mix the juice squeezed from the membranes of both fruits with a little honey to create a sauce. Garnished with mint and julienned orange skin, this makes a delightful dinner dessert with a slice of sponge cake or cookies.

2   seedless navel or blood oranges (8 to 10 oz. each)
2   Ruby Red grapefruits (1 lb. each)
2   tablespoons honey
2   tablespoons julienned orange skin, for garnish
    Mint leaves, for garnish

1) With a vegetable peeler, remove about 6 strips of peel from one of the oranges and cut the strips into a fine julienne. Cut the peel (including the white pith underneath) from the oranges and the grapefruits.

2) With a sharp knife, remove the orange and grapefruit segments from between the membranes, and then squeeze the membranes into a bowl to release the juices. (You should have 1 cup of combined juices.) Whisk the honey into the juice until combined.

3) Arrange alternating segments of orange and grapefruit in four dishes and pour the sweetened juice over them. Garnish with mint leaves and julienned orange peel. Serve cold.

Yield: 4 servings

FIGS VILLAMORA

This is a great snack food, very high in fiber and terrific with a glass of sweet port wine from Portugal, some Gorgonzola cheese and a loaf of crusty bread.

1 **pound (about 24) dried Mission figs (dark)**
48 **whole unpeeled almonds**

1) Split the figs in half starting at the base, but leave them attached at the stem end. Split each half in half again in the same way, and gently press the figs, skin-side-up, on the table. (They should look like flowers or four-leaf clovers with each "petal" or "leaf" still attached at the stem.)

2) When all the figs have been split and pressed, make a sandwich with 2 figs, pressing them together, flesh against flesh. Then, push the almonds, rounded ends first, about ⅓ of the way into the figs where the "petals" connect near the stem, and press to ensure that the almonds are held securely.

3) Spread the fig "flowers" on a tray, and place the tray in a 350° oven for 20 minutes to brown the almonds and dry the figs (which concentrates their flavor).

4) Let cool and then store in a container, tightly covered, until ready to serve. They will keep for up to 2 weeks.

Yield: 4 to 6 servings

FROM VILLAMORA, PORTUGAL Villamora is a town in the southern part of Portugal where you can find dried figs prepared like this in the market. To facilitate the shaping of these, try to get the largest dried figs that you can find. The figs are partially split, spread out, and "sandwiched" together with almonds inserted in the corners. These are then dried in the oven to concentrate the taste of the figs and brown the almonds.

CALIMYRNA FIGS IN SPICY PORT SAUCE

This is a nice combination because you have the sweetness and intense flavor of dried figs complemented by port wine. However the sweetness of the wine is lessened somewhat by the bitter Campari, whose flavor is enhanced by cayenne pepper. (Pictured on page 139.)

1 pound (about 20) dried Calimyrna figs

1½ cups water

1 cup port wine

¼ cup Campari aperitif

Dash cayenne pepper

1 teaspoon cornstarch dissolved in 1 tablespoon water

1 cup plain yogurt

1) Stand the figs in a large saucepan and add the water. Cover, bring to a boil over high heat, and boil gently for 5 minutes. Add the port, Campari, and cayenne pepper, bring back to the boil, cover, and boil for another 5 minutes.

2) Stir in the dissolved cornstarch, mix well and return to the boil. Remove from the heat and cool the figs in the cooking liquid.

3) To serve, divide the yogurt and spread it on to six serving plates. Arrange the figs on top of the yogurt, 3 or 4 to each plate, and spoon some cooking liquid over them. Serve.

Yield: 6 servings

CALIMYRNA FIGS
The name "Calimyrna" is an acronym used to describe a variety of figs grown in California but native to Smyrna, Turkey. When dried, these are pale yellow or beige and have a thicker wall than Mission figs, which are jet black. I poach them here in water, port wine and Campari, that delightfully bitter-tasting aperitif from Italy. When the mixture has cooled and the liquid around the fruit thickened a little, the figs are served with this natural sauce and yogurt, lower in calories than sour cream.

· DESSERTS ·

FRESH FRUIT WITH MINTED APRICOT FONDUE

Colorful and multi-textured, this fruit fondue makes an excellent party dessert. Each guest dips pieces of fresh and dried fruit in a sauce made of apricot preserves, minced mint leaves and kirschwasser, a cherry brandy. You can also flavor the sauce with rum, cognac, or even whiskey, if you prefer, or eliminate the alcohol altogether. (Pictured on page 142.)

Apricot Dipping Sauce

1   cup apricot preserves
2   tablespoons kirschwasser
1   tablespoon minced mint leaves
1   tablespoon water

1   ripe Anjou or Bartlett pear
    (about 7 oz.)
½   pound (8 large) strawberries,
    rinsed, hulled, and halved
2   teaspoons lemon juice
1   large seedless orange, peeled,
    halved, and each half cut into
    ⅜-inch slices
12 dried Calimyrna figs
⅓   cup dark Muscat raisins
8   to 10 mint leaves, for garnish

1) In a small, attractive glass serving bowl, mix together the preserves, kirschwasser, minced mint leaves and water. Set aside.

2) Peel the pear and cut it into fourths. Remove and discard the seeds. Place the pear, strawberries, and lemon juice in a bowl and toss gently to coat the fruit.

3) At serving time, arrange the bowl of dipping sauce in the center of a platter and surround it with the fresh and dried fruits. Sprinkle with mint and serve, encouraging guests to dip the fresh fruit in the sauce.

Yield: 4 servings

· DESSERTS ·

From top: Calimyrna Figs in Spicy Port Sauce and Almond Cake with Mango Coulis.

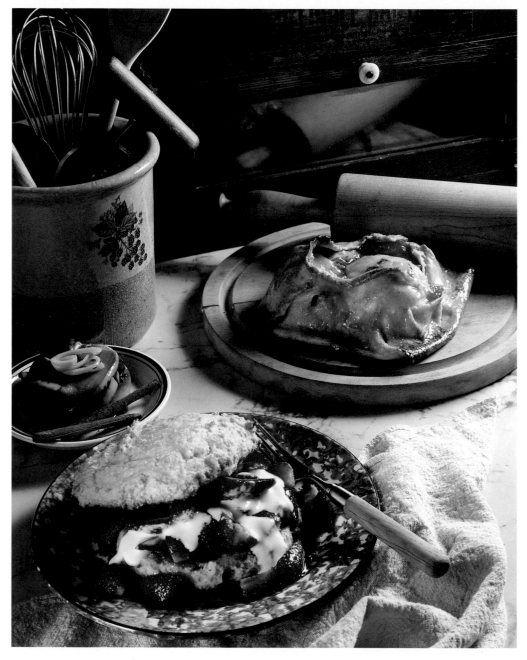

Clockwise: Baked Apple Tart; Strawberry Buttermilk Shortcake and Caramelized Apple Timbale.

· DESSERTS ·

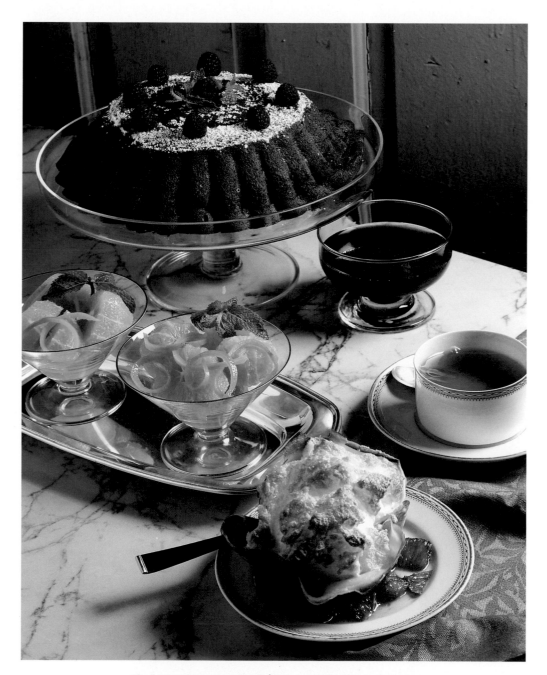

Clockwise: Chocolate Soufflé Cake with Raspberry-Rum Sauce;
Crepe Soufflé in Grapefruit Sauce and Oranges in Grand Marnier.

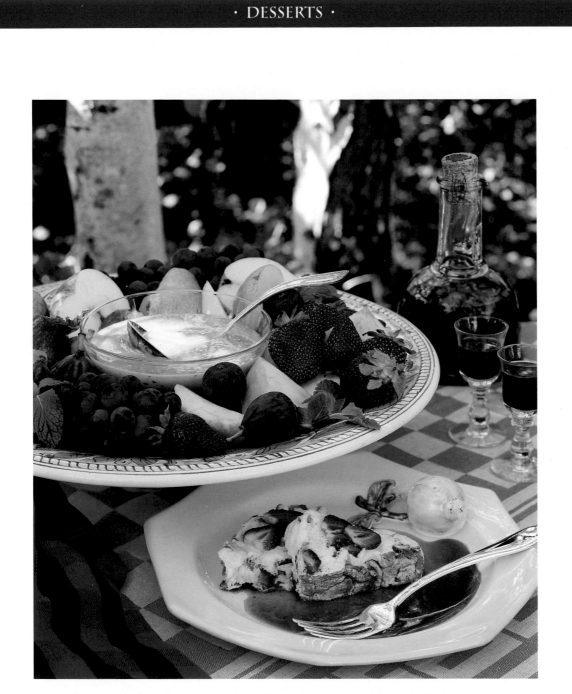

Fresh Fruit with Minted Apricot Fondue and Pistachio Floating Island with Blackcurrant Sauce.

GRAPES & RAISINS IN LIME COOKIE CONES

Here is an impressive, make-ahead dessert worthy of any occasion. A crispy, lime-flavored cookie, rolled up into a cone, is filled with a simple mixture of grapes, dried currants and orange juice. (Pictured on page 2.)

Cones

1 tablespoon unsalted butter, melted

1 tablespoon canola oil

1 egg white

½ teaspoon vanilla extract

1 teaspoon grated lime rind

3 tablespoons all-purpose flour

3 tablespoons sugar

Confectioners' sugar, for decoration

Filling

2 cups (about 10 oz.) seedless Red Flame grapes

⅓ cup dried currants

2 tablespoons orange juice

MAKING COOKIE CONES
For this recipe to work well, it is important to use a heavy, non-stick cookie sheet. Using the underside of a spoon, spread the batter out on the sheet until it is very, very thin; you should almost be able to see through it. As the cookies emerge from the oven, wrap them immediately around a cone-shaped mold (or coated paper drinking cup) until they firm. If allowed to cool, rewarm them briefly in the oven to soften before attempting to wrap them around the mold, otherwise they will crack.

1) Preheat the oven to 375°.

2) Whisk together the melted butter, oil, egg white, vanilla, lime rind, flour and sugar until smooth.

3) Spoon 1 tablespoon of batter at four equally-spaced intervals on a non-stick cookie sheet or parchment-lined aluminum cookie sheet. Using the back of a spoon in a circular motion, spread each mound of batter until it is very thin and has been extended to a diameter of at least 5-inches. Bake until nicely browned (some areas will be browner than others), for about 7 to 8 minutes.

4) Using a large spatula, immediately lift off the cookies and wrap them, one after another, around a cone-shaped metal mold (mine is 4-inches long and has a opening diameter of about 4-inches). Remove each cookie as it firms around the mold and cool the cones on a rack.

For filling:
1) Cut the grapes in half and place them in a bowl. Add the currants and orange juice. Set aside.

2) To serve, dip the open end of the cone in confectioners' sugar, if desired, and arrange on each plate. Spoon about ½ cup of fruit on each plate, so that it appears to be emerging from the cone.

Yield: 6 servings

HAZELNUT PARFAIT WITH CANDIED VIOLETS

This hazelnut parfait, or *parfait aux noisettes,* is an ideal party dish because it can be made well ahead of serving. It keeps frozen for several weeks and advantageously replaces ice cream. Since it serves 6 people, each person gets only about 3 tablespoons of cream, which makes it an acceptable choice for special occasions.

¼ teaspoon canola oil

1 cup (about 6 oz.) hazelnuts

1¼ cups heavy cream

2 tablespoons granulated sugar

½ teaspoon vanilla

3 crystallized violets or other candied or crystallized flowers

1) Preheat the oven to 400°.

2) Grease a 3-cup soufflé mold with the oil. Cut two long, narrow strips of parchment paper and position them in the mold so they form a cross in the bottom and extend up over the sides. Place a round of parchment paper in the bottom of the mold. (The paper strips and round will facilitate unmolding.)

3) Arrange the nuts on a cookie sheet and place in the preheated oven until lightly browned, about 8 minutes. Transfer the hot nuts to a clean dish towel and rub them in the towel to remove as much skin as possible. (Don't worry if half the skin remains.) Place the nuts in a food processor and process until chopped, but not too fine.

4) Whip the cream with sugar and vanilla until firm and then fold in the nuts. Transfer the mixture to the greased mold. Bang the mold firmly on the table to tighten the mixture and eliminate air bubbles. Cover with plastic wrap, pressing on it to flatten the top of the parfait. Place in the freezer for 4 to 5 hours, or longer.

5) At serving time, unmold the soufflé onto a serving plate by pulling gently on the paper strips to help release it from the mold. Crumble the crystallized or candied flowers on top and cut into wedges to serve.

Yield: 6 servings

ORANGES IN GRAND MARNIER

Make this refreshing dessert far enough ahead so that the oranges can cool completely in the cooking syrup. Notice that I use some of the julienned orange rind in this dish, blanching it first to eliminate bitterness. It intensifies the taste and lends texture to the dessert. The oranges are poached just briefly and flavored with Grand Marnier. (Pictured on page 141.)

4   seedless navel oranges (6 oz. each)

¼   cup granulated sugar

2   tablespoons Grand Marnier
    Additional julienne orange peel, for garnish
    Mint leaves, for garnish

1) With a vegetable peeler, cut 2 long, very thin strips of orange peel, each about 1-inch wide, from each orange. Cut the strips into a julienne (very thin strips) place the julienne in a saucepan and cover with 2 cups of water. Bring to a boil, drain in a colander, rinse under cool water, and return the julienne to the rinsed saucepan with 1 cup water and ¼ cup sugar. Cook for 3 to 4 minutes, until large bubbles form and the mixture becomes a syrup.

2) Meanwhile, peel the oranges, removing the white pith under the skin as well. Cut the oranges in half crosswise and add to the syrup. Cover and cook over low heat for 3 to 4 minutes, checking occasionally and adding 1 or 2 tablespoons of water if there is no liquid visible in the pan.

3) Let the oranges cool in the juice and then add the Grand Marnier. Arrange oranges and some juice into each dessert dish. Garnish with additional orange julienne and mint leaves, if desired, and serve.

Yield: 4 servings

CREPES SOUFFLES IN GRAPEFRUIT SAUCE

These crepes can be made ahead and served unstuffed on their own, with the grapefruit sauce or with jam. In this recipe, I fill them with a low-calorie soufflé mixture made from a combination of stiffened, slightly sweetened egg whites and grated lime rind. This same mixture could be baked

Grapefruit Sauce

1	Ruby Red grapefruit (1 lb.)
¼	cup grenadine syrup
1	tablespoon lemon juice

Crepes

½	cup flour
1	egg
¾	cup milk
2	tablespoons canola oil
⅛	teaspoon salt
¼	teaspoon granulated sugar

Extra canola oil for greasing skillet

CLASSIC TECHNIQUE
I use a very light crepe batter which contains only one egg and the crepes are made in an 8-inch skillet. Perhaps the most important thing to remember when making crepes is to spread the batter very quickly in the hot skillet or it will solidify before it coats the bottom of the pan; then, more batter will be required and the resulting crepe will be too thick. Use a twisting, tilting, and shaking motion to move the batter quickly over the surface of the pan, coating it lightly.

1) Grate the grapefruit (colored skin only) to obtain 1 tablespoon of rind. Set aside.

For grapefruit sauce:
1) Peel the remainder of the skin from the grapefruit. With a sharp knife, remove the flesh segments from the surrounding membranes. Squeeze the membranes to obtain ½ cup of juice.

2) Cut the segments into ½-inch pieces (½ cup), and combine in a bowl with grapefruit juice grenadine and lemon juice.

For crepes:
1) In a bowl, mix flour, egg, and ¼ cup of the milk with a whisk until very smooth. Add the remainder of the milk, oil, salt, and sugar, and mix well.

2) Lightly grease the bottom of an 8-inch non-stick skillet and place over high heat. When hot, add 3 tablespoons of batter and tilt and shake the skillet quickly until the batter covers the entire bottom of the pan.

3) Cook for 45 seconds, turn, and cook for 30 seconds on the other side. Continue making crepes, stacking them on a plate as they are made.

without the crepes in a large greased soufflé mold (1½ or 2-quart size) for approximately 30 minutes and then served with the grapefruit sauce alongside. (Pictured on page 141.)

Soufflé Mixture

5	egg whites
¼	cup granulated sugar
1	tablespoon grapefruit rind, from grapefruit above
1	teaspoon unsalted butter
6	mint leaves, coarsely chopped, for garnish

For soufflé mixture

1) Preheat oven to 375°.

2) Beat the egg whites until firm. Add the ¼ cup sugar and the reserved grapefruit rind all at once, and beat another 15 to 30 seconds.

3) Lightly grease six 1½-cup ovenproof glass bowls with the butter. Line each of the bowls with a crepe and spoon the soufflé mixture into the center. Fold the edges of each crepes up over the soufflé mixture to enclose.

4) Arrange the bowls on a baking tray and place in the preheated oven for 8 minutes.

5) To serve, unmold the soufflés and arrange them browned side down (or up, if desired) on individual plates. Spoon some sauce. around each soufflé and garnish with mint , if desired.

Yield: 6 servings

SALPICON OF PINEAPPLE

Salpicon means "to dice" and this dessert consists of diced ripe pineapple that is seasoned with creme de Cassis, cognac and brown sugar. Pineapple is high in potassium, Vitamin C, and iron and ripeness is important here. If you are fortunate enough to find a particularly sweet pineapple, cut down on the sugar. The dark raisins add color, providing a nice contrast to the pineapple.

1	ripe pineapple (3 lbs.)
¼	cup creme de Cassis
2	tablespoons cognac
3	tablespoons light brown sugar
1	tablespoon dark raisins

1) Trim the pineapple at both ends and cut it lengthwise into quarters. Cut out the core. Cut each quarter in half and remove the wedges of fruit from the skin. Cut each wedge into eight pieces.

2) In a bowl, combine the pineapple pieces with the creme de Cassis, cognac and brown sugar. Refrigerate until serving time.

3) Spoon into dessert bowls and serve, very cold, garnished with the raisins.

Yield: 6 servings

BAKED PEARS WITH FIGS

Replace the figs with raisins, if you prefer, or just bake the pears alone with the citrus juices, butter and apricot preserves. This dessert is particularly good when the pears used are ripe and flavorful; the best choice would be those grown on an organic farm. Serve at room temperature.

2	ripe Anjou pears (about l lb.)
16	dried Black Mission figs (8 oz.)
1	tablespoon orange juice
1	tablespoon lemon juice
¾	cup water
1	tablespoon unsalted butter
½	cup water
1	tablespoon apricot preserves
½	cup sour cream (optional)

1) Preheat the oven to 400°.

2) Peel, halve and core the pears. Cut the figs crosswise into slices, and arrange them in a gratin dish. Place the pears, flat side down, on top of the figs and sprinkle them with the orange and lemon juices and then pour in the water. Dot with butter, and spoon the preserves on top of the pears.

3) Bake the pears in the preheated oven for 45 minutes, checking occasionally to ensure that the mixture stays wet so it doesn't burn; if it gets too dry, add a couple of tablespoons of water.

4) Let cool and serve at room temperature with some sour cream, if desired.

Yield: 4 servings

PISTACHIO FLOATING ISLAND WITH BLACKCURRANT SAUCE

This elegant dessert must be made ahead so it can be cold and set before being unmolded. In this recipe, I make it in a loaf pan but it can be made in a round pan, too. Except for the small amount of butter used to grease the baking pan, the dessert contains no fat and amounts to only about 200 calories per serving. The colorful, easy-to-make sauce combines two distinct flavors–strawberries and blackcurrants. (Pictured on page 142.)

½ teaspoon unsalted butter

5 large egg whites (¾ cup)

½ cup granulated sugar

⅓ cup coarsely chopped shelled pistachio nuts

2 large strawberries, hulled and cut into ¼-inch dice (⅓ cup)

Sauce

10 ounces strawberries, hulled

½ jar (10 oz.) natural black-currant preserve (with berries)

2 tablespoons creme de Cassis (blackcurrant liqueur)

2 or 3 strawberries, sliced, for garnish

2 tablespoons chopped pistachio nuts, for garnish

1) Preheat the oven to 350°.

2) Grease a 6-cup loaf pan with butter. Beat the egg whites until stiff, and then add the sugar all at once and beat for a few seconds. Fold the pistachios and the diced berries into the beaten whites, and transfer.the mixture to the loaf pan.

3) Place the pan in a bain-marie and surround it with warm water from the tap. Bake in the preheated oven for 30 minutes, then remove the pan from the bain-marie and allow it to cool on a rack. The dessert will deflate slightly. (The recipe can be prepared to this point up to one day ahead, covered with plastic wrap, and refrigerated.)

For sauce:
1) Slice 2 or 3 strawberries for use as a decoration, and set them aside. Place the remaining strawberries and preserves in the bowl of a food processor, and process until puréed. Add the creme de Cassis.

2) At serving time, unmold the dessert on a rectangular platter. Sprinkle with a little sauce and decorate with the reserved sliced berries and crushed pistachios. To serve, divide the remaining sauce among six dessert plates, and top with a slice of the cold floating island.

Yield: 6 servings

RASPBERRRY GRANITE

Especially attractive when served in champagne glasses, this fresh-tasting sherbert is flavored with raspberry brandy and garnished with mint sprigs. It makes a perfect finish to an elegant meal. (Pictured on page 2.)

¾   **pound fresh raspberries or 1 package (12 oz.) frozen unsweetened raspberries**
1   **cup raspberry preserves**
1   **tablespoon fresh lemon juice**
4   **teaspoons raspberry brandy**
4   **sprigs fresh mint**
     Additional raspberries, for garnish

1) Place the berries and preserves in the bowl of a food processor and process until puréed. Strain through a fine strainer into a bowl. (Yield: 2 cups.)

2) Add the lemon juice and mix. Place the bowl in the freezer for about 2½ hours. The mixture should be hard set but still soft enough in the center so it can be mixed.

3) Transfer the purée to the bowl of a food processor and process for about 20 seconds. (It will "whiten" slightly.) Return the purée to a bowl and place it back in the freezer for another 2½ to 3 hours.

4) To serve, scoop into glass dishes and spoon a teaspoon of the raspberry brandy over each serving. Decorate with a sprig of fresh mint and a few berries, if desired.

Yield: 4 servings

EASY-TO-MAKE GRANITE
This granité can be made with fresh raspberries or frozen raspberries that are packaged without sweetening agents. I add a little lemon juice and raspberry preserves to intensify the taste of the berries and sweeten the mixture. The resulting pureé is frozen, lightly emulsified in a food processor, and then frozen again. This dessert is best served when just hard enough so that you can scoop it out to form a large "curl."

BUTTERMILK STRAWBERRY SHORTCAKE

Homemade strawberry shortcake is a hit with just about everyone and this very easy recipe is no exception. The shortcakes are served with a garnish of sour cream, although yogurt would make a good, lower-calorie substitute. (Pictured on page 140.)

1	pint strawberries
½	cup strawberry jam

Shortcakes

½	cup all-purpose flour
½	cup cake flour
1	teaspoon baking powder
½	teaspoon baking soda
1½	tablespoons sugar
3	tablespoons unsalted butter, softened
½	teaspoon granulated salt
⅓	cup buttermilk

½	cup sour cream
4	sprigs mint, for garnish

A WORD ABOUT SHORTCAKE
In this recipe, I use both baking powder and baking soda. Baking powder is made from a mixture of baking soda and cream of tartar (tartaric acid); I use baking soda in addition because of the sourness and acidity of the buttermilk. It is important that you mix the ingredients for the shortcakes lightly and quickly, combining them just enough so they hold together. Then, press them out on a tray with plastic wrap and cut them into squares, so there is no waste.

1) Rinse and hull the berries. Cut off about ¼-inch from the stem end of each berry. (This part of the berry tends to be less sweet, especially if the berries are not completely ripe.) Reserve these trimmings for the sauce. You should have 2 cups of trimmings and 2 cups trimmed berries.

2) Cut the trimmed berries into wedges and place them in a bowl. Transfer the trimmings to the bowl of a food processor. Add the jam to the berry trimmings and process until smooth. Pour the sauce over the berries, toss well and set aside in the refrigerator for at least 1 hour, or as long as 6 hours.

For shortcakes:
1) Preheat oven to 450°. In a bowl, combine the flours, baking powder, soda, sugar and salt with the butter, mixing gently with a spoon for 30 seconds at most. (The mixture should not be completely smooth.) Add buttermilk and mix with a spoon just enough to combine the ingredients into a soft dough. Invert the dough onto a non-stick cookie sheet and cover it with a piece of plastic wrap. Press on the dough until you have extended it to a thickness of about ⅜ inch, and then cut it into 2½-inch squares. Bake in the preheated oven for 10 to 12 minutes. Remove to a rack; cool.

2) At serving time, cut the shortcakes in half horizontally. Arrange bottoms on four dessert dishes and spoon berry mixture on top. Cover with the shortcake tops, and garnish each with sour cream and a sprig of mint. Serve.

Yield: 4 servings

· DESSERTS ·

CANDIED ORANGE RIND

This is an inexpensive treat, using only sugar and orange skins. The skins can be made ahead over a period of days and set aside in the refrigerator until candied. The candied rind will keep for several weeks or until needed, if stored in an airtight plastic container. It should be dry on the outside, but moist and chewy inside.

2   large seedless navel oranges
    (1¼ lbs.)
1⅓ cups sugar

1) Trim off both ends of the oranges and cut through their skin lengthwise in six equally-spaced places. With a sharp knife, remove the skin and pith underneath. If the cottony pith is very thick, remove some of it from the skin, holding your knife horizontally. The rind should not be much thicker than $\frac{1}{16}$ inch; if thicker, it will take longer to cook.

2) If you have a vegetable peeler that cuts deeply, use it to remove $\frac{1}{16}$-inch strips from the skin. Pile up the skin sections, and cut them into strips about ½-inch wide. You should have about 3 dozen strips.

3) Place the strips in a saucepan, cover with 6 cups cold tap water, and bring to the boil. Boil for 5 seconds, drain, and rinse under cool tap water. Return the strips to the washed pan with 1 cup of the sugar, and add 6 cups of cold tap water. Bring to the boil, and boil over high heat for about 1 hour, until the rind is almost transparent and the syrup is just beginning to darken and become like caramel. Remove from the heat.

4) Spread the remaining ⅓ cup sugar on a cookie sheet. With a fork, transfer the orange peel strips to the tray and press them into the sugar to coat on all sides. Arrange on a plate and allow to dry for 1 hour, then transfer to an airtight container for use as needed.

Yield: 3 dozen pieces

BLANCHING THE RIND
Be sure to blanch the rind well and then wash it before placing it back in the saucepan to cook in the sugar–it will be too bitter otherwise. Make sure that the pan has been cleaned before the washed rind goes back in!

· POSTSCRIPTS ·

· NUTRITION ·

Changing Nutritional Emphasis in the '90s

To me, modern cuisine is really common sense cuisine. Today's menus should consist of foods that are tasty and beautiful, as well as include a variety of foods that help to maintain healthy weight. They should be low in saturated fats and cholesterol, contain plenty of vegetables, fruits and grain products, and include sugars, salt and alcohol in moderation.

Techniques & Equipment

I have found that using certain techniques and equipment in the kitchen can enhance the nutritional value of our foods. For instance, fats are the most calorie laden food that we eat. With few exceptions, any reduction in our fat intake will improve our diets.

One excellent way to cut down on the use of fats in cooking is to use non-stick pans. The amount of fat that is used to saute in non-stick is less than half of what might be used in a nontreated pan. I like to use non-stick pans with a permanent finish when I saute and fry.

Also, grilling is a great way to enhance the flavor of foods, and cook them without the addition of extra fats or sodium.

There is great diversity in the types of grilling units available today. When I grill, I like to use natural wood chips such as apple wood, olive wood or cherry wood for their delicious smoky flavor and ability to produce high heat. I often use wood charcoal because it is pre-cooked so it turns to hot coal more quickly. Charcoal briquettes are petroleum based and should be reduced to a grey-ash color before cooking. This reduces the tar flavor that can be picked up from them.

Vitamins & Minerals

For years, we have been concerned about the level of vitamins and minerals in our diets. Modern cooking has given us some new insight into this old subject.

We now know that the old way of cooking vegetables, which was to blanch them in large pots of boiling water and then refresh them in cold water before seasoning, resulted in the loss of essential vitamins and minerals. I recommend cooking vegetables in a small amount of boiling water just until the water disappears, thus retaining the maximum amount of vitamins and minerals.

Also, iron is a particular concern for many people, especially women. Many of my recipes, such as Moules Maison (page 60), Clam Croquettes (page 48), and Beans & Broccoli de Rapé (page 34) are high in iron.

Protein

Red meat, long maligned as a high fat protein source has moved into the 90's as a much lighter main course item. Now that beef and pork are being raised to produce leaner meat, we can get our iron and protein from these red meat sources without worrying about fat intake. By trimming the meat properly before cooking, and serving smaller portions, red meat is part of a healthy gourmet diet.

Fiber

Today, experts recommend a diet high in fiber to help reduce cholesterol. For you and me, that means approximately 25 to 30 mg. of fiber per day. Luckily, water soluble dietary fiber is contained in some delicious packages. Fiber is a part of plant foods. It is found in abundance in whole grain breads and cereals, vegetables, fresh and dried fruits and vegetables, or peas and beans like those found in the Cauliflower in Scallion Sauce (page 100), Figs Villamora (page 136), and Quinoa with Sunflower Seeds (page 79).

Complex Carbohydrates

Complex carbohydrates, which give us long lasting energy by slowly converting to sugars during digestion, do not necessarily need to be combined with high fat foods to be delicious. Complex carbohydrates are found in many of the foods which also happen to be rich in fiber, vitamins and minerals such as whole grain breads, cereals, pastas, rice, beans, and potatoes.

Calories

Reducing calories does not necessarily mean eating tiny portions of trendy food. There are many hearty, filling dishes that you can prepare and consume knowing that they are very low in calories. I have included some of these dishes in *TODAY'S GOURMET.* They are: Grilled Chicken with Cabbage Anchoyade (page 70), Poulet au Pot (page 75), Sautéed Scallops with Snow Peas (page 54), and Salmon Pojarski (page 62).

I have suggested several dessert recipes that are quite low in calories, too. While a typical portion of dessert often contains as many as 500 calories, the following desserts are much lighter and contain about one-third the calories: Pistachio Floating Island with Blackcurrant Sauce (page 150), Raspberry Granité (page 151), and Chocolate & Fruit Nut Cups (page 131).

During the holidays, we all tend to consume a few extra calories that we might not eat during the rest of the year so I have suggested a holiday menu that is not only delicious, but contains approximately one-half of the calories of a normal holiday feast. The menu features Sautéed Scallops with Snow Peas (page 54), Roasted Turkey with Mushroom Stuffing (page 80), Carrot Purée with Ginger (page 103), Chocolate Mint Truffles (page 132), and Candied Orange Rind (page 153).

· POSTSCRIPTS ·

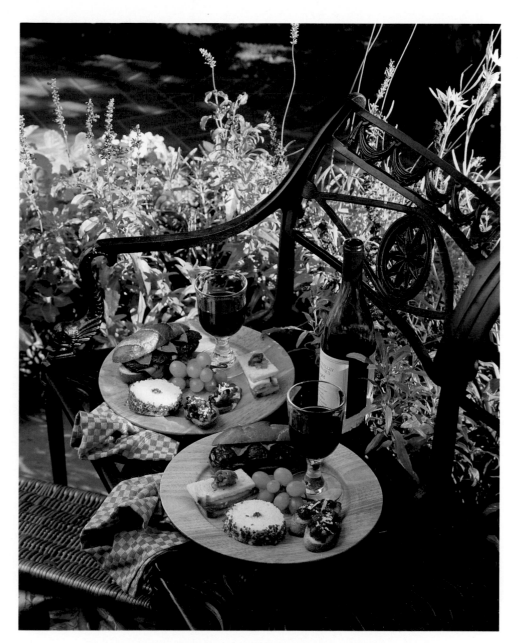

Rear plate: Roasted Eggplant Sandwich; Salmon & Cucumber Sandwich;
James Beard's Onion Sandwich and Olive & Tomato Toast.

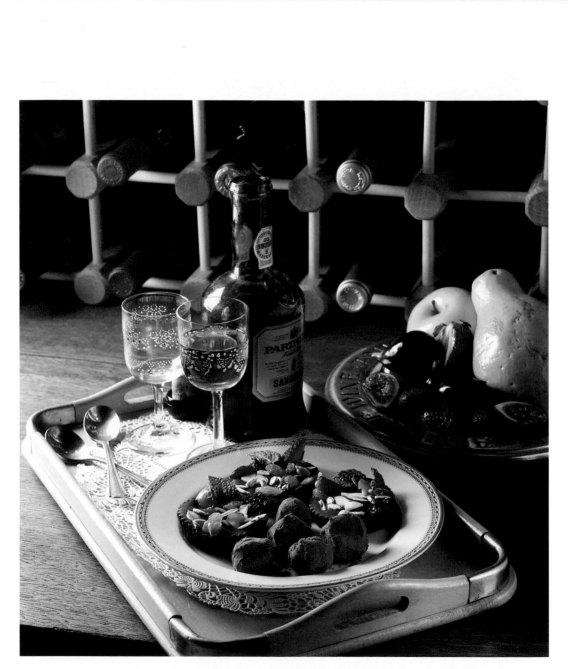

From top: Seasonal Fruit; Chocolate & Fruit Nut Cups and Chocolate Mint Truffles.

· NUTRITION ·

Cholesterol

The American Heart Association recommends that we consume 300 mg. or less of cholesterol per day. In most instances, I use oils instead of butter to cut down on cholesterol. In addition, I have created breakfast recipes which minimize the number of egg yolks that an individual consumes.

Fats & Fat Substitutes

Experts believe that a healthy diet is one where no more than 30% of the daily calories consumed are derived from the intake of fat. To achieve this percentage, I sometimes make low fat substitutions in my recipes. For example, non-fat or low-fat yogurt may be substituted for sour cream.

Some fats have been proven beneficial. Salmon, although it is a fatty fish, contains what is now described by experts as "heart healthy fats" or Omega 3's. These Omega 3's help keep blood from getting "sticky" and forming clots which lead to heart attacks. Fatty fishes have also been known to lower that fats in blood (called triglycerides). Because of these benefits, health experts are urging us to eat more fish, up to 15 pounds per year.

Sugars

It is important to remember to use moderation when consuming refined sugar. Refined sugar can lead to tooth decay, and when combined with fat, can be tremendously caloric. But, who can resist sweet treats during the holidays? For this reason, I included recipes for small chocolate truffles (page 132) and Chocolate & Fruit Nut Cups (page 131). A small bit of richness can help you to feel satisfied without overdoing it.

We often eat too much sugar for breakfast, too. Why not eat a savory, high-protein breakfast suggested in the menu on page 19?

· NUTRITION ·

Salt & Sodium

I have some special tips to cut down on salt. Because I like highly seasoned foods, I use a variety of seasonings as salt substitutes. Tabasco sauce, plenty of fresh herbs and strong-flavored spices are excellent substitutes.

The key to reducing the amount of salt used in cooking is to bring up the natural flavor in the food itself. For example, if you crystallize the juices on the outside of meat before cooking it, you can bring up the flavor without adding salt. Another way to enhance flavor is to use citrus such as lemon or lime, or any number of fresh herbs and spices available today. And don't forget about flavor-enhancing cooking techniques such as grilling, steaming or broiling.

Vegetables

Vegetables are the most important kind of food to emphasize in our diets. They are naturally low in calories, and high in fiber, vitamins and minerals. Whenever possible, I buy organic fruits and vegetables for their fantastic flavor and guaranteed wholesomeness. My friend, Alice Waters of Chez Panisse Restaurant, says that by purchasing organic fruits and vegetables, we support the people who work to preserve and enhance our farmlands.

When I was young, my mother was an organic gardener, and she didn't even know it! But this was in a time when organic farming was not a specialty, it was a way of life.

Grains

Adding whole grains to your diet is a great way to add protein, fiber, and complex carbohydrates. I often use traditional grains like Cream of Wheat, (the center of the wheat berry) and oats in non-traditional ways. My Chicken & Spinach Velouté (page 27) and Oatmeal Leek Soup (page 31) are

· NUTRITION ·

good examples. Also, I recommend using grains that are just now gaining in popularity like quinoa, featured with grilled quail on page 79.

Oils

In today's supermarket, you will find a vast selection of oils. I think that it is important to understand the nature of oils, in order to know which one to choose. For instance, some oils are lower in saturated fat than others, some are more strongly flavored, and some may even burn at a relatively low temperature, giving off bad odors and flavor.

At room temperature, all oils are liquid fat. Some oils, like palm oil, are very high in saturated fat and therefore can boost the level of blood cholesterol. In much of my cooking, I try to use the oil that is lowest in saturated fat–canola oil.

Extra virgin olive oil is usually dark, with a rich olive flavor. The color and flavor is the result of olive solids that are present in the oil. Extra virgin olive oil is so named because it has been removed from the olives by mechanical pressing, from the sheer weight of the olives. No heat or chemical processes are used to extract this oil. These olive solids which impart flavor and color burn at fairly low temperatures. So, extra virgin olive oil is best used for salads and marinades.

The best oils for use in sautéeing are flavorless safflower, canola, or, for mild flavor, peanut oil. These oils are ideal for sautéeing because they can withstand high temperatures without burning.

· NUTRITIONAL CHART ·

	Calories	Protein (gm.)	Carbohydrates (gm.)	Saturated Fat (gm.)	Cholestrol (mg.)	Sodium (mg.)
Almond Cake with Mango Coulis	254	6	30	2	67	29
Asparagus in Mustard Sauce	82	2	3	.51	0	387
Baked Apple Tart	263	2	41	6	27	3
Baked Apricots with Almonds	101	2	18	1	4	7
Baked Bananas in Lemon-Rum Sauce	217	2	52	.05	0	5
Baked Pears with Figs	248	2	57	2	8	8
Beans & Broccoli de Rapé	313	18	40	2	12	731
Beef Carpaccio	269	19	3	5	47	485
Blueberries with Brown Sugar	110	2	25	.28	2	28
Braised Pork Cocotte	248	27	11	3	72	277
Braised Sour Cabbage	178	3	38	1	4	443
Braised Stuffed Artichokes	300	5	25	3	.54	578
Broccoli Piquante	90	3	6	.96	0	167
Brown Rice Chicken Fricassee	324	16	46	9	54	828
Buttermilk Bread	404	13	67	5	23	420
Calimyrna Figs in Spicy Port Sauce	250	4	60	.54	2	38
Candied Orange Rind	90	.11	23	0	0	0
Caramelized Apple Timbales	168	.36	37	2	8	2
Carotte Ciboulette	73	1	11	2	8	477
Catfish on Ratatouille	458	38	11	5	115	682
Cauliflower in Scallion Sauce	112	2	5	1	.08	154
Cherry Bread Pudding	241	5	42	2	8	85
Chicken & Seafood Paella	626	29	53	10	166	868
Chicken & Spinach Velouté	175	3	19	5	27	446
Chicken in Tarragon Sauce	215	28	5	4	107	377
Chicken Legs with Wine & Yams	433	43	32	3	155	462
Chicken Broth	40	48	5	0	0	1

· NUTRITIONAL CHART ·

	Calories	Protein (gm.)	Carbohydrates (gm.)	Saturated Fat (gm.)	Cholestrol (mg.)	Sodium (mg.)
Chocolate & Fruit Nut Cups	176	3	19	6	0	2
Chocolate Mint Truffles	157	3	14	7	54	6
Chocolate Soufflé Cake with	349	6	37	10	78	54
Raspberry-Rum Sauce	—	—	—	—	—	—
Clam Croquettes	282	9	9	3	24	340
Coffee Creme Caramel	122	6	16	2	66	75
Corn & Pepper Sauté	129	3	17	4	16	149
Cornmeal au Gruyère	148	6	17	3	16	323
Couscous of Lobster	568	33	59	3	82	782
Crab Cakes with Avocado Sauce	325	13	7	4	63	522
Crepe Soufflés with Grapefruit Sauce	206	6	27	2	41	118
Croque Monsieur	317	17	20	7	47	656
Curried Bulgar with Currants	190	5	34	.53	0	281
Figs Villamora	288	5	61	.67	0	11
Fresh Fruit with Minted Apricot Fondue	286	4	85	1	0	13
French Fries	278	4	36	2	0	12
Fricassee Claudine	385	18	44	8	66	177
Garlic Soup	289	6	36	3	9	651
Grapes & Raisins in Lime Cookie Cone	134	2	24	1	5	11
Gratin of Scallions	189	11	31	3	14	239
Grilled Chicken with Cabbage Anchoyade	520	57	11	4	135	1228
Grilled Savory Lamb Chops	171	19	.45	3	61	328
Grilled Leg of Lamb	279	37	8	4	114	346
Grilled Quail with Quinoa	178	17	2	3	00	46
Hazelnut Parfait with Candied Violets	369	5	10	13	68	20
Hot Shrimp on Greens	236	21	4	.2	140	328
Irish Lamb Stew	271	26	27	4	74	502

· NUTRITIONAL CHART ·

	Calories	Protein (gm.)	Carbohydrates (gm.)	Saturated Fat (gm.)	Cholestrol (mg.)	Sodium (mg.)
James Beard's Onion Sandwiches	279	4	25	3	13	484
Jam Sandwiches	222	2	28	3	56	44
Leeks with Tomato & Olive Oil	272	7	41	2	0	470
Moules Maison	295	19	18	2	37	680
Mushroom Omelet	280	10	13	14	290	282
Mushroom-stuffed Potato Pancakes	195	2	18	1	0	439
Mushroom Stuffing	161	3	22	.80	.49	277
Mussels Gratinee	336	18	19	11	130	711
Oatmeal Leek Soup	224	11	27	5	30	384
Oeuf Cocotte	165	8	14	3	220	262
Olive & Tomato Toasts	318	6	26	3	3	983
Oranges & Grapefruit Segments	136	2	35	.01	0	2
Oranges in Grand Marnier	127	.88	29	.03	0	.12
Pan Bagna	467	15	73	2	7	1575
Pasta & Zucchini	275	8	35	2	2	236
Pasta with Fresh Vegetable Sauce	343	10	42	16	44	632
Peas à la Française	161	5	20	.98	0	675
Pistachio Floating Island with	196	5	35	.62	.85	47
Blackcurrant Sauce	—	—	—	—	—	—
Pommes Anglaises	127	3	28	0	0	12
Pommes Persillade	176	3	21	2	8	79
Potage de Leǵumes au Vermicelli	227	6	39	1	4	569
Potato Crepes with Caviar	519	25	20	10	538	1256
Poule au Pot	501	45	58	4	121	1365
Poulet au Vin Rouge	421	47	21	3	144	708
Purée of Carrot with Ginger	136	2	16	1	2	473
Ragout of Rabbit	409	44	7	22	131	508

· NUTRITIONAL CHART ·

	Calories	Protein (gm.)	Carbohydrates (gm.)	Saturated Fat (gm.)	Cholestrol (mg.)	Sodium (mg.)
Raspberry Granité	277	1	68	1	0	11
Red Snapper in Potato Jackets	381	32	20	19	52	491
Roasted Eggplant Sandwiches	514	16	60	25	22	402
Roasted Turkey	474	78	5	13	219	421
Salmon Pojarski	243	23	13	10	55	681
Salpicon on Pineapple	127	.52	25	.50	0	3
Saucisses au Chou on Lentils	449	26	27	27	65	997
Sautéed Eggplant Rolls	475	11	23	40	24	756
Sautéed Salmon on Greens	361	31	9	23	78	517
Sautéed Scallops with Snow Peas	190	16	8	11	36	280
Smoked Pork Roast with	159	21	4	2	41	1047
Mustard-Honey Glaze	—	—	—	—	—	—
Smoked Salmon & Cucumber	250	17	32	5	32	453
Sandwiches	—	—	—	—	—	—
Smoked Whitefish Mold	180	12	13	9	36	550
Spicy Beef Shell Roast	238	31	1	31	87	219
Split Pea Soup with Cracklings	373	21	49	11	13	754
Steamed Cod on Tapenade	359	29	9	24	65	1274
Steamed Endive with Lemon Juice	55	2	6	3	8	148
Strawberry Buttermilk Shortcake	404	5	63	15	37	526
Tomato, Onion & Parsley Vinaigrette	133	4	9	19	10	188
Trout Sauté Terry	438	38	7	29	116	844
Tuna Tartare on Marinated Cucumbers	249	27	4	14	43	737
Turnips & Mashed Potatoes	151	3	22	6	15	304
Veal Chops with Mushrooms	305	30	6	18	120	404
Veal Roast with Artichokes	340	42	20	10	168	578
Wine Merchant Steak	382	44	7	18	117	689

· INDEX ·

· INDEX ·

· INDEX ·

· INDEX·

· INDEX ·

· INDEX ·

· T ·

· INDEX ·

The best collaborations have an air of effortlessness about them, but it is rarely achieved without a great deal of effort from many quarters. That's certainly true of making a television series, and KQED's collaboration with Jacques Pépin benefitted from the remarkable assistance of friends of the station and of Mr. Pépin, many of whose contributions may not have been apparent on the screen but which I'm happy to recall now. A hearty thank you to all of the companies who provided production assistance:

Campton Place Hotel, San Francisco
Rent-A-Computer, San Francisco/
  Santa Clara
Bourgeat USA
Harvey Antiques, San Francisco
Crate & Barrel
Greenleaf Produce, San Francisco
Chantal Cookware
Corning, Inc.
Rowoco
Wüsthof-Trident
General Electric
Thermador
Forrest Jones, Inc.
Pierre Deux

La Parisienne Antique Posters
Chantry/Charlotte Clark Ltd.
Edgecraft Corp.
Norton Co.
Dvorson's Food Service Equipment Co.
  (Distributors of Wolf Ranges)
Dandelion
Macys California, Inc.
Kobrand Corp.
Krups North America
Cuisinart Corp.
Bragard, Inc.
Cost Plus, Inc.
JB Cumberland & Associates
Nicolazza & Associates

In addition, many individuals helped make the series a joy to produce. Thanks to:

Jan Birnbaum, chef at Campton Place, for producing with alacrity a variety of unreasonable requests such as non-reflective champagne buckets and larger-than-life catfish; Bill Wilkinson and Anya Ushakova, for providing a true home-away-from-home for our guests; Charlie van Over, for a certain *je ne sais quoi* on our Connecticut shoots; Stephanie Turner, for excellent and down-to-earth nutritional information; our on-camera guests, Merle Ellis, Alice Waters, Martin Yan, and Claudine Pépin, for their enthusiasm and patience in the studio; Michel Scheinmann, Hans Rathsack, Geri Given, Terry Burns, Forrest Jones, Coco Jefferson, Matt Meyer, Dick Chasin, Cornelius O'Donnell and Donna Keegan, who went beyond all expectations in providing cookware and tableware; Emily and Toby Harvey, who made available their delightful collection of furniture and antiques; the staff and students of both the California Culinary Academy and the French Culinary Institute, for providing the backbone of our back kitchen; Norma Galehouse, Mr. Pépin's tireless assistant, who was the indispensable "binding ingredient" in this cross-country concoction; and Gloria Pépin, who not only put up with six months of production demands on her family, but literally put up the production crew in her house.

Peter L. Stein,
Producer

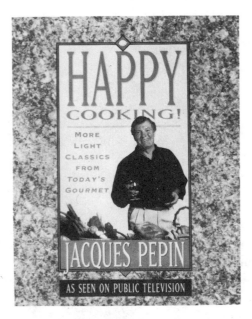